SUNNY SIDE UP!

An inside look at early morning T. V.

By: Ann Varnum
WTVY-TV's Talk Show Hostess
LaVa Publications
Webb, Alabama

Dedication:

To the loving memory of my father, J. P. Jones, who said "You can do anything you want to do if you want it badly enough and are willing to work for it."

And to my fraternal grandmother, Annie Jones, who always believed in me, no matter what, and loved me unconditionally.

Loving thanks to my mother, Elizabeth Jones, my husband Jerome Varnum, my three sisters; Becki Haston, Martha Lavallet, and Paula Leatherwood; my children: Trant and Karen Bullard, Paige and Andy McCallister, Steve Varnum; my grandchildren: Brandi, Amber, Matthew, Nicholas and Cassidy; and all my fellow co-workers at WTVY who still put up with me.

Information About the Author:

Ann Jones Varnum (Mrs. Jerome Varnum) received her B. A. Degree in Speech and English from Huntingdon College, Montgomery, Alabama. She did her graduate work at Auburn University, Auburn, Alabama in English and taught in Alabama schools for a number of years. As the TV Talk Show Hostess for WTVY's "Morning Show", Ann once held the position of having the longest running talk show with the same hostess in the state. Today, she does her interviews as part of WTVY 's News 4 This Morning. Ann is also the Public Affairs Director of WTVY.

Ann and her husband Jerome are active members of First Presbyterian Church in Dothan, Al and work with Meadow Wood Inc., an out-door Christian adventure camp.

In 1971, Ann was diagnosed with systemic lupus erythematosus at Ochsner's Foundation Hospital in New Orleans, Louisiana. Miraculously, she has not suffered a major flare up of the disease since then. In early July 1994, Ann started her 24 year stint on WTVY-TV as hostess of "The Morning Show".

The following was written about Ann Varnum by a retired Methodist minister Rev. Charles A. Cornell in a letter to her Aunt Lula Boswell.

December 26, 1943

Dear Lula,

I have had my heart stolen away by Ann Jones, 4 years old. She is such a very sophisticated child, a natural born actor and singer. I was enchanted. You, of course, know her so you can imagine what happened to a lonely old preacher now entering his 80th year.

I said, "Ann, I want a lock from your golden hair to put in the back of my watch, and keep, for you are going to be a writer, author, a Metropolitan Star, or a Movie Queen some day." She said, "Maybe I will!" I cut it and we put it in. "Now," I said, "when you become famous, I can say, 'I knew her when!'" I am crazy to have her visit me in my home. She casually remarked to "Bud Daddy", who was reading her a story teasing her, "You would not be kidding me, would you Bud?" Can you beat that for an aside; soto voice? Such airy graces, such goo eyes, such posturing! She even watches herself cry in the looking glass. Is she a "Throw Back" or a genius unheralded, unannounced, or unknown as yet from some far distant Boswell of Scotland or England to rival the Boswell who immortalized himself by writing the biography of Ben Johnson and is now remembered for that exquisite piece of writing, while Johnson is well-nigh forgotten? I know not. But, Elizabeth and J. P., as I call him, has a problem child upon their hand and hearts.

I only wish, as I have plenty of this world's cash I might guide the events of her life for she will make hearts turn upside down in love or despair, in pleasure or sorrow for she is a marked child of genius now and here.

Rev. Charles A. Cornell

Note From the Author:

This book is written from my heart. It is not supposed to be great literature because it is told simply, pretty much like I talk. I hope it will not only be an encouragement to you, the reader, but will also inform you and hopefully entertain you! With me, what you see, is what you get. God Bless you all!

Prologue

Change is always inevitable and although I usually resist change, I have learned to be flexible in order to grow. I was not prepared, however, for the first mention by our station manager of the possibility of canceling our "Morning Show".

There had been so many changes already. Taking a vehicle like "The Morning Show", moving it to a new time and calling it "Morning Talk", removing my co-host Gary Bruce and fellow co-worker Teresa Thomas and changing the whole concept of everything I was used to programming had been difficult enough, but now, there was the definite possibility of our program being totally canceled

Linda Scott, a delightful sunny blonde had been anchoring from Panama City for half of the program for the new "Morning Talk"; and, in truth, we were really beginning to work together very well:

"Ratings", our boss kept saying, "You just don't have them anymore! You have the senior citizens but you don't have the 18-35 age group that we target."

"Nine o'clock is a difficult time slot for that age group.", I tried to explain, but the station manager had so many problems to consider that I knew I had very little to say in the matter.

Ultimately, it was decided that "Regis and Kathy Lee" would take "Morning Talk's" time slot in September, and I was instructed to program the show (which was now cut back to 30 minutes and re-named "The Morning Show" without the Panama City segments) until the first of September.

So, I did what I always do. I prayed. "Father, put me where you want me to be. If I'm supposed to stay on the air, I will, and if you want me somewhere else, then it is fine with me. I want only your perfect will for my life."

There had been no mention of my being let go; in fact, just the opposite. I was going to be allowed to do "on air news stories and features", and I was to continue as WTVY's Public Affairs Director.

Soon word leaked out that the show was going to be canceled, and I received a number of job offers. None seemed right for me, however. Then a set of circumstances began to develop that I can only describe as totally miraculous! Our station manager decided to cancel our "Morning Show" in August instead of September; therefore, I had to call and cancel the guests that I had scheduled for the remainder of August. I asked our boss what to tell my guests and he said, "Tell them 'The Morning Show' is being canceled." I did exactly that.

I was overwhelmed with the response of our viewers. There were protesting phone calls, letters, letters to "The Dothan Eagle", articles in the papers and talk radio did a long feature on what was happening. Ratings or not, the people of our area wanted "The Morning Show."

About the very same time, CBS offered us local time slots during their 7-8 a. m. "CBS This Morning". John Michael worked with our station manager to format my program into those time slots and "WTVY News Four This Morning" became the new vehicle I was given to do my interviews.

On Friday, August 22, 1997, "The Morning Show" as a regular program ended. We did some old clips, had a few tears and was visited by a very happy boss who had finally reached a decision that worked for everyone. He was the one who announced that I wasn't going anywhere but would be back on Monday at a new time. (Which, by the way, was the original time that I had initially started doing the program all those years ago.)

On August 25, 1997, I came on at 7:00 a. m. in the morning on "WTVY News Four This Morning." Truly, as the Lord had already spoken in my heart, "I didn't miss a beat!" And, by the way, the ratings each new rating period have been higher than ever in all age groups.

Contents

Chapter   **Page**

1   The early days with Co-host Rex Roach........1

2   WTVY News Director Bob Howell joins
    me in the mornings..............................9

3   Don Day, D. J. from WTVY-FM swaps out
    with Bob Howell................................19

4   And then there was Tony Scott................32

5   Tough on the outside, a softy at heart- Chris
    Bence..52

6   And back comes Tony Scot....................72

7   On the road.......................................89

8   The time between..............................108

9   Tom Nebel joins me and Teresa Thomas on
    "The Morning Show"..........................124

10 Gary Bruce, the total professional, Co-hosts
    "The Morning Show" with me................146

11 WTVY moves to downtown Dothan.........157

12 Changes, changes, changes...................170

13 WTVY-TV News Four This Morning.......187

14 Miscellaneous memories.....................198

15 Excerpts from letters and memos...........217

In the beginning...

It seems like yesterday in some ways, and forever ago in other ways, but I remember when I first knew that I would someday do a program like "The Morning Show". Actually, I don't guess it registered in my mind until much later, but I do remember the day I was told what was to be my destiny.

It was a very bright spring morning, and I had to get up early in order to be on WTVY's "Morning Show" with two of my favorite people, Betty Gault and Bob Peterman. I had been on the program before as President of the Dothan Service League and had many times shared my vision for the beginning of the Girls Club in Dothan. This particular morning, however, I was to do a "live commercial" for a jewelry store that we owned.

Getting up early has never been one of my strong points as I, by nature, am a "night" person. I groaned as I struggled to get ready. "I can't believe anyone can get up this early on a regular basis", I complained. "This certainly isn't for me!"

At last, I got ready, drove to the station, and was greeted by two delightful co-hosts, Betty and Bob. They really did everything to make me feel at home and help me relax. Betty did a few announcements, and then, the two of them did an interview, and it was time for me. I was really nervous. I had my speech, some props and a collection of our better watches. As I was introduced, I ad libbed through my spot, put a man's watch on Bob and held a ladies' watch for Betty to look at. It was only two minutes in length but it seemed like an eternity. The table we sat behind seemed to "wobble" at all the wrong times.

Afterwards, Betty and Bob very kindly assured me that I had done really well, but I was not sure at all.

It was later, as I left the old WTVY building on Highway 52 East and was driving into town, that a thought "popped" into my mind. "Someday, you'll be doing this full time!" I remember shaking my head and pondering, "Now, where did that come from?"

Later, through some very unusual events, I was offered a "Morning Show" position at WDHN, the ABC affiliate in Dothan, but two things stood in the way. Number one, I would never be willing to go in competition against the greatest lady ever, Betty Gault, and secondly, I was diagnosed with lupus erythematosus that year and spent the entire summer of 1971 recuperating at Ochsner's Foundation Hospital in New Orleans...Someone else got the job.

Chapter One
The early days with Co-host Rex Roach

I started working for WTVY in 1974. Charles Woods had bought the station and had canceled the very popular "Morning Show" with Bob Peterman and Betty Gault. He never dreamed he would receive so many complaints!. The public outcry was great, but by then, Betty Gault had already left WTVY.

To answer the community demand, Mr. Woods assigned Rex Roach the task of putting together a new "Morning Show" with a co-hostess for the new program. Jennifer Roach, Rex's wife, attended my ladies' Tuesday morning Bible class that I held in my home, and she had mentioned to Rex (without telling me) that I would be perfect for the job. Rex was not very enthusiastic about this idea at first.

One day someone named "Ann" called Rex to inquire about the job. The deadline for applications was nearing and because Rex was in a conference at the time he promised to call her back. When he returned the call...you know what happened...it was me he called, thinking, obviously, that Jennifer had mentioned the opening to me.

When I told him I had not been the one who called and that I didn't know anything about the "Morning Show" job, he was really surprised. "Well", he began, "someone named 'Ann' called me and I thought it was you." Then, he began telling me about the job and encouraged me to come out to the station and see about it. (We found out later that another Ann had really made the initial call.)

I was still in shock when my husband, Jerome, suggested that I apply for the job! "Why, Honey" he encouraged, "I really think it would be good for you!"

That did it! It was no longer a joke but a serious prospect. A strange excitement began to well up inside. How could anyone know that I had secretly desired all my life to do a television show? Jerome and I prayed about the entire matter, and I promised the Lord that I wanted only His will to be done and that I wouldn't be disappointed if I didn't get the job.

After doing the initial taped interview with Rex Roach, I felt I had really messed up. Jerome consoled me by saying, "Now Ann, you're always so hard on yourself. You probably didn't do as bad as you think!"

The next day, Rex called. "Ann" he began, "I've got some bad news for you."

I interrupted with, "Oh, that's all right, Rex, Jerome and I prayed about it and we only want what is best."

Rex broke it, "No, you're wrong… the bad news is you 're going to have to start getting up early!"

I had gotten the job!

During the first few weeks of planning "The Morning Show", I tried to quit several times. There was just so much more to the job than I had anticipated. Mr. Charles Woods, owner and general manager of WTVY, was very understanding about my health situation and assured me that I could rest when I needed to and leave in time to get a nap in the afternoons before my children got home from school. There was just so much to learn!

Rex was a real pro, and he helped me work on my make-up. On television, the natural looking cosmetics I usually wore simply would not do. The circles under my eyes seemed magnified, and, of course, I looked at least 10 pounds heavier on TV.

At the end of our first show, I was truly relieved that I had held up under the pressure. "Thank you, Lord," I breathed silently, "That's <u>one</u> show down!" Helen Youngpeter from Wiregrass Mental Health and Huntley Johnson, a local attorney, who played some musical instruments, had been our first guests. That was July 29, 1974.

The people at WTVY were always patient and very helpful. "Smile more, Ann", they encouraged. "Just be yourself on TV and you'll be fine." At the end of the first week, we received one very complimentary note which stated, "I like The Morning Show with Rex Roach and Ann Varnum !" Since it was unsigned, we were not sure if it had been Rex's Mom or mine who had sent it. Another note, in contrast, was signed and it read, "I want to see the CBS News instead of "The Morning Show." I think the two of you would do better on a Kiddie Show!" Rex only laughed and said, "If this is the worst criticism we get, we'll be lucky."

"Sheer terror" is the only way to describe the way I felt during the first "live" commercial I did. No one told me that I was going to have to do a commercial that morning. Phil Bump, one of our cameramen, told me to go over and stand under the lights on another set to see how he should line me up. Phil made a funny motion (I learned later this meant, "You're on!") and there I was...with nothing to say because I didn't have any copy! I just stood there and smiled while I'm sure thousands at home were

3

urging, "Say something, Ann! Say something!" But, for once in my life, Ann didn't have anything to say.

Oh, there were other "bloopers". I sometimes walked in front of the cameras at the wrong time, interrupted guests in the middle of their sentences and once, I accidentally said, "limited quality instead of limited quantity" while doing another live commercial! Wow! Did I have a long way to go.

Rex and I learned how to work together very soon, and we lightened our format to include: a visit to the re-created 1850 pioneer village of Westville, Georgia, (where Rex played a century old piano); a ride on a circus elephant (Rex topped my act by mounting his elephant carrying the camera on his back to record the sensation of being on top of an elephant.); and an encounter with a "bull-whip" champion who had worked with Lash LaRue. I was a little nervous about being "whipped", and my mother almost fainted when she watched the show.

One morning Rex did not come to work. He was usually there early to prepare the news and weather which he did as part of our program. By the time we discovered that Rex had been involved in an accident on his new motorcycle and had broken his collar bone, it was too late to call anyone else to do his part of the program.

Randall Barnes, our director, said, "Ann, you'll have to do it!"

...I stammered, "I can't do the news and weather, I've never done it before!"

"Well," he said, "you'll just have to try, there is no one else."

Phil Bump, my cameraman, went with me hurriedly to the newsroom and pulled the news feed and weather off the machine. I rushed back to the set (in my belted white turtle neck sweater which topped my red and white flared leg pants) and I stood there and somehow managed to make it through the weather. I've never been good with geography, but I did the best I could with the pointer and the map. After the weather, I rushed back to my guest, did the interview and then back to the news set. We didn't have a teleprompter or anything. In those days it was simply, "rip and read!" That's what I did. Bob Howell had told me once, "If you aren't sure of yourself, pretend you are and no one will know the difference."

This was a day to test all of my acting skills. I really faked it. When the show was over, Randall said, "I surely hope Charles Woods wasn't watching today."

I gasped, "Oh, was I really that bad?"

He smiled and said, "No, you were really that good, and if he thinks you can do both jobs he'll want to save money by having one person do the show!"

Everyone at the TV station teased me the rest of the day. Jerry Vann, one of our news men, proceeded to "imitate" the way I had done the weather in my flamboyant red and white flared pants. We really had some good laughs.

I learned a big lesson that day: "Never take yourself too seriously."

A very popular continuing feature that Rex and I had developed during our time together was the "Encounter" segment. These in-depth studies dealt with an area of public affairs or community concerns, like trips to schools for "special" or handicapped children; a tour of the local rehabilitation center; life in the Houston County jail; an overview of special heart disease detection equipment; and a day in the life of a state trooper (filmed with real perception by WTVY's Jerry Vann)

Jerry later told us that we had tried to get him killed because during the night filming, the state troopers had been involved in a high speed chase with Jerry and the camera bouncing along in the back seat! The footage, nevertheless, was excellant.

One of the highlights of my first year at WTVY was interviewing famous author and Pulitzer Prize winner James Michener. Attorney Alto Lee had brought Mr. Michener out to our studio for the interview, and I must admit I was "star-struck!" Rex, being the seasoned interviewer, took the lead during our conversation with my questions sprinkled in.

When I took Mr. Michener up to meet our station manager, Mr. Charles Woods. I thought I had adequately prepared Mr. Michener for Charles Woods (explaining how Mr. Woods had suffered terrible burns during World War II), but I had not prepared Mr. Woods for the literary giant James Michener! I introduced the two of them, and, immediately, Mr. Woods piped up with, "Now, Mr. Michener, what is it you do?" I was mortified, but I shouldn't have been. Mr. Michener and Alto Lee had a good laugh about his question, and Mr. Woods apologized by explaining that he really wasn't much into reading.

Rex and I did a lot of "just for fun" things together. I remember covering still another story in Lumpkin, Georgia, at the 1850 Village of Westville. One of the costumed tour guides discovered, to her dismay, one of the Village's cats in the process of having kittens on one of the antique beds, which was covered with an embroidered one hundred year old coverlet. She immediately took her cane to try to force the cat off the bed, and I, being the animal lover that I am, grabbed the cane and begged her not to do it.

"Please don't hurt her," I exclaimed, "she's is in labor!"

At that point, Rex nearly dropped the camera because he was laughing so hard. Thank goodness, the dear lady agreed to allow one of the housekeepers to gently remove the mama cat and put her in a box. (Mercifully, too, Rex had run out of film before my grand gesture!)

One of my most remarkable feats was performed (to my great surprise and Rex's too) when Kent Swicegood, a public affairs director at Ft. Rucker, brought out a target pistol and an outlined target to demonstrate the proper way to protect yourself. Rex dared me to shoot the pistol at the target. I did, and put all five bullets through the target man's heart!

"Folks," they exclaimed! "Don't mess with this lady!" In reality it was either blind luck, or my guardian angel. I kept the target for years.

Once, we had closed down the set for the day and cut off all the lights when I realized I had left my format folder on the coffee table. As I entered the somewhat darkened studio, I was startled by a costumed wrestler, "The Wrestling Pro", who was sitting in my chair waiting to do a car commercial. Naturally, I was not expecting to see anyone, so I screamed. The poor man jumped up and began to protest that he wasn't going to hurt me. "Miss, I'm just an actor!, he blurted out. It was so funny because I couldn't convince him that I was not afraid of him but merely surprised to find a living human being sitting there. I really don't think he ever believed me.

Another memorable event was going on location to the Olympia Spa to interview Barry Goldwater, Jr. I had really gone all out to dress up for the occasion. Jerry Vann was to do the filming for me. I know now that Jerry and our city mayor Jimmy Grant had plans to tease me a little because they told Senator Goldwater that I had named my cat Barry Goldwater after his father. The Senator just beamed and said, "That's swell!" I guess that ruined their joke on me!

...

As Rex Roach tells it, one of his most exciting moments came when he took his wife Jennifer to Birmingham to do an interview with recording artist Pat Boone and Christian business leader George Otis. Rex and Jennifer were backstage at the precise moment Pat and George stepped off the stage. Not only did the interviews go off without a hitch, but the two men that Rex had come to meet, spent time sharing their Christian faith with him.

God really did a work in Rex when as he came to realize that he could no longer bargain with God. It was at this point that he decided to turn his entire life over to the Lord. Not long after Rex made this decision, he left WTVY to go into an advertising firm. Today, he is a marketing developer for Deep Rock Inc. in Opelika, Alabama. Rex and Jennifer have two grown sons.

Chapter Two
WTVY New Director Bob Howell joins me in the morning.

Next, Bob Howell, News Director at Channel Four, joined me in the mornings. Even though I had grown up with Bob (like Rex) in our hometown of Geneva, Alabama, I had to get used to Bob's different temperament and personality. It was not long before the questions we both addressed to our guests flowed smoothly. Each knew what the other was about to do before the other one did or said anything.

I'll never forget our very first interview together. It was to be taped around 1:00 p.m. with a very prominent mayor of a north Alabama city. This man was not only a very controversial figure at the time, but threats had even been made against his life. When he arrived at WTVY, he was accompanied by two armed bodyguards. Before the interview, he went into the men's room to freshen up. Twenty minutes passed, then thirty, then forty-five minutes. Fearing a problem, one of the guards knocked on the door. We were all afraid that something had happened to him inside that small men's room. Evidently, he was all right, because approximately an hour and a half later he emerged so that we could do the interview. (I will always wonder what he was doing for that length of time.)

Bob Howell was, and still is, one of the most professional people I've ever had the privilege of working with. He got his early training at our local radio station, WGEA in Geneva, and after coming to WTVY, had worked on the earlier version of "The Morning Show" with Bob Peterman and Betty Gault. He taught me so very much.

For example, on one occasion a number of us were supposed to do a car commercial together. I had only two lines to deliver as I perched on the hood of the car. Suddenly, the actress in me took over. It was awful. Very kindly, Bob tutored me into speaking in a natural tone and not like I was on stage. His help was invaluable to me.

Not only did Bob do "The Morning Show" with me, but he anchored the six and ten o'clock news and was WTVY's News Director. To top it all off, on Saturdays, he acted as the Master of Ceremonies for WTVY's live wrestling programs which we broadcasted then directly from our studios.

These events were unbelievable! The wrestlers often borrowed razors from our art supplies to cut themselves in their scalps so that they would readily bleed. Seeing blood caused the fans to go wild.

Bob would entertain us each Monday morning with these colorful stories about the antics of the wrestlers. One time he told us how "André, the Giant", had accidentally knocked out a fellow wrestler by plowing the poor man's head into what André thought was a flimsy prop. In reality, the plyboard had been attached to a concrete wall instead.

In another incident, Jerry Vann was running camera for wrestling when a wrestling bear jumped out of the ring and headed straight for him. Jerry, to protect himself, abandoned his camera, only to discover that all the bear wanted was the RC Cola that Jerry had placed beside the camera.

•••

There was the time that Bob and I interviewed Barry Saddler, who had written the song "The Green Beret". He had come by the station early one morning on his way to Florida. I was really disappointed in him, though, because he was a very bitter man who had turned totally against our government. (What would John Wayne think?)

•••

One day when I came to work, I discovered that the front door to the station was still locked and that no one could find the key. My first guest, Peggi James, the local president of the NAACP, came up to the door but I couldn't let her in. I simply asked her to go around to the back. She refused, by saying, "I worked too hard to be able to come in the front door, and I'm certainly not going to the back!" Because of her tone, I thought she was serious; Peggi was only kidding. We have been dear friends ever since.

Soon after Bob and I started doing the show together, Margaret Thompson, a newspaper columnist for *The Dothan Progress*, wrote the following about us. Excerpts from the article are reprinted here by permission:

"I would like to be Racquel Welch, but somehow I always turn out to be Carol Burnett!!"

That statement was made by Ann Varnum, who with Bob Howell, WTVY's news director, are the personable hosts of a smashing show that hits the airwaves

11

at an appalling 7:15 each morning. Is all the early-morning cheer that's beamed into frantic, rushing households really faked?...It's not, as you can see if you've ever ventured into the world of Ann and Bob on their Morning Show set. Their friendship goes far beyond a camera's range. They grew up together in Geneva, Alabama, sharing many good times and many ups and downs. It was a warm reunion when they became co-hosts of the "Morning Show." They have learned to laugh at themselves and put everyone around them at ease. If a guest is late arriving - or if there's panic on the set for any number of reasons – the dynamic duo have a knack for covering up. And if there's no way to cover up, so what? They make the most of it and usually have fun at the same time.

Ann's zest for living stems from a near - fatal illness in 1971.

"I had a rare blood disease, lupus erythematosus and the doctors said it was incurable," she said, "There's a purpose for my being spared, and I want to share my feelings with the world."

...

Dothan's own Bill Espy, "Snapper" and Jim Houghon, "Greg" from CBS's soap opera *The Young and the Restless*, paid us a visit. Fans had heard that they were going to be on our program, so they had filled the parking lot at our station for a chance to see the stars. I remember one very pregnant lady who timidly came inside to use our restroom. She was all dressed up in party clothes with rhinestones and sparkly sandals. In view of the fact that she had waited for hours, she must have been very uncomfortable.

My heart went out to her as she shyly glanced over at her heart-throbs! Seeing the lady standing there, Jim Houghton, jumped up, took her by the arm, unlocked the studio door and escorted her to the lobby. I will always appreciate his kindness to her, and I'm sure she'll never forget it either.

···

Bobby Goldsboro, whose song "Honey", was a big hit, came back to town, and the city rolled out the red carpet for the Dothan native. There was a big celebration at the Dothan Civic Center, and Bob and I enjoyed doing interviews and acting as co-hosts for the event.

Later that same year we met Billy "Crash Craddock", Jeannie Pruitt, and O. B. McClinton. It was interesting to discover that celebrities are usually very nice and totally approachable.

···

Guy Lombardo was coming to town, so Bob and I sponsored a contest for a lucky couple to get to meet Mr. Lombardo as his honored guests. Pharmacist George Hammond and his wife won the contest and were elated over getting to meet the famous conductor.

Bob planned to meet me backstage that night, as I was scheduled to do the interview. Was I ever surprised when I approached Mr. Lombardo's brother (who was actually NOT his twin but a mirror duplicate of Guy) to interview him. The only difference in the two was that Mr. Lombardo had on a black tuxedo while his brother wore a red band suit. The two of them were very congenial, and I was impressed with the ease in which Guy Lombardo answered my questions.

...

To keep our viewers up-to-date on new entertainment opportunities, Bob and I interviewed a local starlet who had been cast in a movie with Burt Reynolds. Innocently, Bob asked her how she had been cast, and did her physical looks fit the character they were looking for on screen? Her mother was very upset about his question, because the young girl had played a teen-age prostitute in the movie. For some reason, the lady thought that Bob had implied that her daughter had been cast because of her "character". Anyone knowing Bob Howell would automatically know that he would never deliberately do anything to insult the young girl. Somehow, we were able to convince the family that they had misinterpreted Bob's question by showing them the tape of the show.

As a means of promotion, CBS had wonderful "Star week-ends" where local affiliates could go and interview the stars of the new CBS shows. I was so excited about getting to attend these events, and confident, because Bob always took care of me. Steve Griffin and David Woods often went along with us, and they always added much to our adventure.

On one such trip, I needed some greenery for the table which was to be used for interviews. David and Steve went out and "borrowed" some plants from the hotel lobby. I was afraid we'd get thrown out, but thankfully, nothing happened.

That week-end, one of the new stars who played the newspaper owner, Mrs. Pynchon, on *The Lou Grant Show* with Ed Asner came for her interview wearing a bath robe with a turban wrapped around her head. As soon as we escorted her to the set, she started eating the plants that Steve and David had procured from downstairs.

"Tasty", she announced, "I haven't had breakfast!" We all thought she was a little strange.

On account of the fact that David's father, Charles Woods, owned our station and because David and Steve delighted in calling me and Bob, "Mom and Dad", word was soon out that Bob and I were married, owned WTVY and had two sons, Steve and David. We really got a lot of attention as that rumor spread among the CBS stars and executives.

Cloris Leachman was a particularly arrogant star. When she came to our suite, one of the poor waiters had just brought her a glass of orange juice. She nearly screamed at the poor man:

"I ordered freshly squeezed orange juice! This is canned!"

The waiter spoke in broken English that he had turned in her order just as she had requested. He was apologizing profusely when she added, "Look, I want freshly squeezed orange juice and nothing else. Money is no object. Just see to it I get my juice!"

At that point I think we all wanted to "slug" her! He next insult involved me personally. She began to tell me how bad my hair looked, how out of style it was, and then, seeing my children's names on a piece of paper, (I had written Trant, Paige and Steve's names down so that the stars could give each of them an autograph), she lambasted my choice of names.

"Why in the world would you saddle your children with those names? They will be ridiculed all of their life!" (And remember, her name is Cloris Leachman!) Bob became so irritated with her that he almost shut the camera down, until I looked at him. In that moment, we both knew that our Southern upbringing would overcome her rudeness. Needless to say, we did a very brief interview with Ms. Leachman, and neither of us ever watched her new show *Phyllis*.

Next in line was Loretta Switt.

"Oh no, Bob," I groaned, " I'll bet she's as bad or worse than Cloris!" Was I ever in for a big surprise! Loretta Switt was the essence of charm and warmth. I had seen her years before in Chicago when she did the stage play *Mame* with Celeste Holm. I had loved her in her role as Agnes Gouch, and she was so pleased that I had enjoyed her so much.

When we told her about Cloris Leachman's antics, she explained to us how disgusted everyone at CBS was with her.

"Why, only last night," Loretta related, "Cloris jumped up on one of the dining room tables and began doing cartwheels with her dress on! I think she's on something or really impressed with herself!"

•••

Our technical ability at WTVY was forever changed when, on another trip to Atlanta for the CBS Star weekend, Bob and I had the privilege of picking up our new video equipment at a local outlet. Up until then, all outside interviews had to be on film . Bob wanted to make sure everything was working properly with the new technology, so that year we video-taped and filmed each star's interview just to be on the safe side.

I'll never forget when Robert Wagner came walking into our suite. He was at least fifteen minutes early, had on the neatest shirt and tie and carried his dark suit jacket over his shoulder by his fingers. He was electrifying! The very first thing he did was very graciously shake all of our hands and introduce himself. Robert Wagner was as fascinated with the new video equipment as we were.

Mr. Wagner's CBS show that year was *Switch.* It was all about a former jewel thief who now worked for the law. In his personal life, he and Natalie Wood had just remarried, and when I brought it up, he just beamed. "Thank God for a second chance!" he said.

(When Natalie Wood drowned in that boating incident much later, I grieved over his loss.)

Right after Robert Wagner left, in walked *Medical Center's* handsome doctor, Chad Everett. He was as nice as Robert Wagner but totally different. Whereas Robert Wagner had been almost shy and a little quiet, Chad Everett was a very noisy and funny extrovert. He loved the new video equipment so much that he hammed it up in front of the camera in order for us to play it back and let him see himself.

Looking at my watch, I realized our time with Mr. Everett was running out (we were only allowed fifteen minutes with each star.) After much effort, we finally got him to sit down for our interview. I had placed a sign over to the right in a chair so that each star could always remember my name. It read, "Hi, my name is Ann".

Well, he got all carried away with that one. He pretended at first that he couldn't see it by squinting his eyes, and then he began to say, "My name is Ann! Gee, I thought my name was Chad Everett!"

I got him off that by saying "Sir, you are so handsome that you can call yourself anything you want to, but I've got to do this interview."

He flashed that gorgeous smile and said, "O. K., I'll behave!" In the few minutes that we had left, he did just that. It was a good interview.

After meeting Robert Wagner and Chad Everett, back to back, as it were, I knew that the rest of my interviews would be downhill. These two stars were big names but they treated all of us with respect. That is not always true of "budding stars or starlets", and especially, not true of all soap opera performers. Some are really difficult to interview because they appear to be stuck on themselves.

One beginning new star never made it to our interview. He had to stop by our bathroom to fuss over his hair. We could hear him moan and groan as his stylist worked to please him. I only remember that his first name was Larry. Our time ran out before he got ready, so we had to send him on his way. It was just as well because the show that he was in was canceled after the first month. To my knowledge, I've never seen him on anything else either.

One important thing I learned while working with my Geneva co-hosts was never go to the movies with Bob Howell or Rex Roach! Every time I see re-runs of the "Pink Panther" series, I remember all their remarks on how all of the stunts were done or how different shots were probably filmed on different days because of the cloud patterns, the sun angles, or the different colored socks worn by the star! Do those two ever know how to analyze a good movie to pieces!

Chapter Three

Don Day, D. J. from WTVY-FM swaps out with Bob Howell

There was a period of time when Don Day (Larry Prevatte is his real name) from WTVY-FM, our country radio station, switched out with Bob for a while. Bob had so many other responsibilities that it was difficult for him to do everything; therefore, he gave up the early morning job at Mr. Woods' request.

Not long after Don became my new co-host, I cooked supper one night for Bob, Rex, Don and their families. We also invited WTVY Sports Director, Al Roberts. My two sons, Steve and Trant, had seen my three co-hosts so much that they were used to them, but Al Roberts, now, that was another matter. Immediately, they wanted his autograph and hung on to his every word all evening. Al was a big star to them! Al got quite a kick out of this, of course.

...

When Ray Stevens came to the Ozark Civic Center, Don and I were scheduled to do an interview with him after the show, and Bob was going to tape it for us. Was I ever disappointed! Off stage Ray Stevens has zero personality. He is "on" when he is on stage and definitely "off" when he isn't performing. At first, I felt that it was all my fault because the interview did not go well. Don and Bob assured me that I had done nothing wrong but that the problem lay with Mr. Stevens' personality. (I believed them, finally, when years later I interviewed him again and the very same thing happened.) You really never know about a performer until you get them away from their area of expertise.

I grew to appreciate Don after we had worked together for awhile. Don's selling point on the air was his "little boy" vulnerability coupled with his good looks. While Bob had always been in command of every situation as expressed by his charming forcefulness and authority, Rex had the knack of knowing a "little" something about everything. Don's appeal lay in "understatement". He had a talent for making "unrehearsed", and, usually, "unthought" through comments! For instance, once when he simply could not pronounce our next guest's profession (an anesthetist), he shrugged and said, "Well, bring on the gas passers!" I had a hard time keeping a straight face over that one!

...

A big thrill for me was the day Sam Elliot walked into our studio! He was in town promoting his picture *Life Guard*. Without a doubt, you couldn't overlook his great good looks, but he was easy to talk with, and I felt the interview went well. It has been gratifying to see how successful he has continued to be as an actor.

...

Robert Urich came to our city to do a promotional campaign for Solomon Chevrolet. In spite of the fact that he was on the ABC affiliate with the program *S.W.A.T.*, we were still able to set up an interview. That Saturday morning was a duzzy! Hundreds of people were packed like sardines into John Solomon's show room. Don and I had to climb over them, in order to do a "stand up" interview with Robert Urich. By the time we got there, he had already signed so many autographs that he was developing cramps in his hand.

Looking up at me he said, "Say, I've seen you somewhere before!"

I quipped right back, "You've probably seen me on television!" That was a great ice breaker, and we had a very good time together. Later, that summer, I got to interview his wife, Heather Menzies, at the CBS Star week-end. She was starring in *Logan's Run* with Gregory Harrison. At that same time Robert Urich had just signed to do the "Dan Tanner" role in *Vegas*. Right after we completed our conversation with his wife, she called her husband, and I got to talk with him over the phone. To say the least, he could never forget coming to Dothan!

...

Meeting Pat and Shirley Boone and their daughters at the Dothan airport was also a big moment for me. Jerry Vann did the taping, and he started with Pat Boone's white shoes as he stepped off the plane and kept the camera there until he panned up for me to do the interview. The Boones were going to perform a big family show at the Ozark Civic Center. When Don and I went to the show, we were so surprised that our viewers seemed as excited to meet us as they were the Boones.

Seeing Don and I together every morning caused some of our viewers to think we were married. In fact, one night as we were covering the National Peanut Festival, one of our elderly viewers took her cane and pushed Don away from his wife.

"I'm going to tell Ann that you're all hugged up on that woman!" she almost snarled. Don tried to explain that he and I were not married, to which she indignantly replied, "I know you are married, too, because I see you every morning together!"

Right after she left, Jerome and I came up, and Don told us about what had happened.

"For goodness sake", Don laughed, "Don't 'hug up' on Ann, because that dear lady might hit you with her cane if she sees you do it!"

...

Don and I had the privilege of doing a number of special projects. One of our favorite programs was filmed at the Rose Hill Day Care and Training Center for Retarded Children. All the young girls would act like they were "swooning" over handsome Don, and he teased with them in good natured fun.

I remember thinking then how very special the teachers at the school were in order to be able to teach these retarded students. They were firm but compassionate; orderly, but flexible. Little did I realize at the time, that one day my own daughter, Paige, would become a "special education" teacher herself.

It was soon after the program at Rose Hill, that we began our Houston County Kiwanis Club Telethon for our area ARC. Although we wanted to bring in just as much money as possible, we also wanted to provide an educational, and, entertaining program. Celebrities from all walks of life volunteered their time and talent.

"Friends", a local choir composed of special children under the direction of Ms. Barbie Nelson always made a guest appearance for us. Also, Bobby Taylor, a student confined to a wheel chair, usually came by to say a few words at the telethons. With his bubbly personality and warm heart, Bobby could always motivate people to call in and give more money. He also demanded a "big kiss" from me each year and would tell everyone that I was his girlfriend.

We also hosted the American Heart Association's telethon to help my dearest friend Betty Ramsey raise money for their special projects. One year Alabama Quarterback, Scott Hunter, co-hosted the show with us. To start the competition, we capitalized on the fact that I am an Auburn fan. Viewers called in pledges to support their favorite school. I gave it my best effort, but, Alabama fans won. I had to say "Roll Tide", as that was the consequence I paid because I failed to raise the most money. We also auctioned off "Bear Bryant" hats and Auburn and Alabama footballs.

Prior to one Heart Association Telethon, the up-and-coming country stars "Alabama" came down and pre-taped some songs for us to air during the telethon. I will always regret that one of our WTVY engineers, not realizing who they actually were, but judging them only by their looks,(long hair, beards, old jeans, etc.) was rude to them and rushed them out of the studio without allowing them to see their tape after they had finished.

...

Don and I also taped a segment together where we got a his and her "uniperm". Don's hair fuzzed out like a balloon and even though mine looked a little better, we decided never to do that again!

With his usual flair for having fun, there was one morning when Don started giving our director, Joe Earl Holloway, a hard time while we were on the air, so Joe put a "big black ball" on Don's head with our new technical equipment. It followed Don wherever he moved until he laughingly apologized to Joe.

Right after getting our unattractive perms, we had a visit from two "Amazons" who had brought a snake show to Northside Mall. When one of the ladies pulled out her big boa constrictor from a burlap sack, the snake headed toward my chair. I immediately jumped for Don's lap! Afterwards, I realized that I had been a little silly, but I had reacted in the only way I knew- "Run baby run!" We all had a good laugh when we remembered this incident.

The very next day, one of the women brought us a huge lizard. It seemed harmless enough until during a break it rolled out it's appallingly long tongue to catch a fly! That really grossed me out. When we came back from the break, this lizard jumped right past my shoulder to get on our trellis backdrop. I couldn't help it! I screamed! One of the women had already told me that these lizards liked to get in people's hair!

Don kept joking with me, "Ann, can't you just get control of yourself?" I really did try to do better after that, but I was never very comfortable with the huge reptile staring at me.

Since sports, (and football in particular) has always been such a big thing in our area, Don and I began our Thursday and Friday Morning sports segments. We would invite a coach and three or so of his players on Thursday, and then, on Fridays, we would host members of the football squad that would oppose the other team that Friday night.

The following article appeared in the Jackson County Floridian by Don Moore, Sports editor concerning our series:

Bulldogs to be on TV while Gulf Breeze gets ready for action

Marianna coach Wendell Davis and three Marianna Bulldogs will appear on Channel 4 Thursday morning at 7 a.m. The program hosted by Don Day and Ann Varnum called the "Morning Show" tries to get personalities from every walk of life to appear on TV. I spoke with Day Tuesday and he said that they attempt to get high school coaches and players from throughout the viewing area for guest appearances. "Some of our most interesting shows are when we schedule opposing coaches. We get their views and points of view on upcoming games," he said. Tune in to Dothan's WTVY Channel Four this Thursday morning at 7 a.m. to see the Bulldogs on TV.

Right in the middle of one of our sports programs, one of the big ol' burly football players who was scheduled to be on that day, told me he was "scared to death," and, that he might faint. I assured him that we would be easy on him. When his time came to be on, I noticed that his face was very pale, and that his knees were buckling. I could just imagine him passing out right then and there. To make matters worse, when he held the hand microphone, he squeezed so hard that he mashed the release button and the cord fell right off the mike. At this, it was obvious he was about to panic. I hurriedly called for a break while we fixed the microphone, but we did let him off the hook. He never appeared on the air again. Poor boy, I am sure his teammates teased him forever.

Don Day always enjoyed the visits from the "49'er Party" at Ft. Rucker, especially the "Can Can Dancers". In those days, we didn't hesitate to do everything "live" so they danced and sang and often messed up Don's hair or sat in his lap. When they left our show to go to breakfast, they always received compliments on the show as well as a lot of stares, too.

The musical Broadway show *Godspell* came to town, and we did what we knew to do, we rolled back the cameras and let our guests sing and dance and do excerpts from their show. The cast of the show really complimented us on how well everything turned out. They could not believe a station in the size market we were in could do what we had done. Don and I always believed Joe Earl, Phillip Bump and our other cameraman, Johnny Williford could and would do anything we needed, and they usually did!

One morning Don and Bob came in all excited about an invitation they had received to be trained by the Ft. Rucker Parachute Club to jump out of airplanes. I protested, "You can't do that! What if you get hurt?" They only laughed, and proceeded with the training.

The day of the initial jump, Jerry Vann covered the story, and his video was hilarious! Bob had a habit of putting both hands together under his chin when he was pondering over something; consequently, in the feature, he always looked like he was praying. Don could be heard in the background voicing his doubts about the jump. When time came for the jump, they both jumped, but Bob sprained his back a little. Don, on the other hand, was fine. Our director, Joe Earl Holloway, muttered that there might be enough men on the ground to "put him in an airplane" but the plane couldn't carry enough men to "toss him out", he added.

...

The Harlem Globetrotters were great fun when they visited us at WTVY. They came out to our show before doing a benefit at Wallace College. Our program got totally out of control! There is absolutely nothing like "live" TV. As there is no way to cover up mistakes while a show is being broadcast. That night at the game, the whole Globetrotter team picked on me and Don and tried to get us up to play basketball with them. (We both declined.) They kept bouncing basketballs all around us even on the bleachers. They surely know how to work a crowd.

...

Dottie Lawrence, as the marketing director at Dothan's new Northside Mall always sent us the greatest guests including mountain crafters from Tennessee, North and South Carolina and other states. These artisans did everything from "scrimshaw" (an art form engraved on whale bones), to paintings on wooden articles. One artist painted me a "purple camel" on a tiny pin. It's one of my favorite pieces of jewelry since purple is my favorite color, and, at the time, I collected camels.

...

To catch an interview with Natalie Cole, the talented daughter of the late Nat King Cole, one Saturday morning, Bob Howell and I drove out to Dothan's Municipal airport to meet her. When we first requested the interview, her road manager pushed us aside and said "absolutely not", but Natalie interrupted with, "Of course, I would love for you to interview me," and we did.

Ms. Cole told us how proud she was to be Nat King Cole's daughter. When I asked her if her father would have approved her choice of careers, she smiled and nodded "Yes."

"Daddy was always proud of me," She added. "I know my singing would have made him happy."

(Unfortunately, Natalie Cole later went through a battle to overcome drug addiction. I'm glad she made it.)

Soon after my interview with Natalie Cole, it was Don's time to have a motorcycle wreck. But unlike what happened following Rex's accident, Don Day was not badly injured. We even got his "spill" on camera, and we show it to him nearly every time he visits us.

Things began to change at WTVY once more when our station management decided to put Bob Howell back on the program with me again. Don was assigned to do the weather at 6:00 and 10:00 on the night news. Don, of course, was very nervous about this new job due to his lack of knowledge about geography. When he mentioned weather fronts, for instance, he would just point in the general area of the map and say that this "front" was coming up over here and moving on over there. Sometimes, when Don ran out of anything to say, he would often make some statement about "doing The Morning Show" and drive our news director crazy! Viewers still loved Don, no matter what he did.

Right after Bob rejoined me on the program, I got an opportunity to interview a very famous country star, Charlie Rich. I was definitely not a country music fan at the time, but I was excited about meeting Charlie Rich at Dothan's airport. Bob and Jerry Vann were both scheduled to join me there. When they didn't show up, I was very concerned because both of them are so reliable. Before long, I learned why they weren't on time. A nice gentleman brought me a message that their car had broken down at a railroad track north of Newton, and that I was to go pick them up. I apologized to Mr. Rich and asked if I could do the interview after his show that night. He very kindly said, "That will be fine".

While looking for Bob and Jerry, I went to where I thought "north of Newton" and a railroad track would be. It was near the fabulous Italian Villa Restaurant, but no Bob and Jerry. I drove for thirty more minutes until, at last, I found the abandoned car near 231 North, but, by then the two of them were gone. They had given up on me and had hitched a ride back to town with a local farmer.

I never did get that interview with Charlie Rich. It is sad to say, but by the second show at the Ozark Civic Center, Mr. Rich was too inebriated to perform. I really started praying for him after that.

...

Bob Howell and I had the pleasure, along with WTVY-TV management, of co-sponsoring "Up With People". The young men and women in the production were very talented, and so energetic that we tried to fit them in on our program every day while they were in Dothan. Performers did every song and dance "live". No one told us we couldn't do it that way.

When my beloved father, J. P. Jones, died on July 6, 1976, Bob had to do the show that week without me. I'll always remember his kind words, and the love and compassion that he and all my co-workers expressed to me during this sad time in my life.

Bob had also been going through some very difficult struggles in his own life and just as we had done with Rex, Jerome and I shared our personal faith in God which had never let us down. One stormy day, as Bob was riding down the highway, he flipped the radio on and heard Elvis Presley singing one of Bob's all- time favorites, "You

Heard Me Crying in the Chapel". The exact timing for that song was just perfect. Bob was so moved by the Holy Spirit that he immediately pulled off the road and told God, "O. K. Lord, if you'll have me, I'm yours."

When Bob called me at home, he was expressing so much excitement that, at first, I thought that he had had an accident. I was overjoyed when I realized the decision that he had made. Not too long after this, Bob moved to Montgomery to work at WSFA-TV. Today, he and his wife, Paula, have two teenage sons. Bob also teaches media courses at Troy State University in Troy, Alabama. Bob Howell is the one who started calling me "Grannie Annie". He said this was a perfect name for me because I always knew everybody's business, counseled with everyone, and loved them much like a grandmother would. Also, Bob said, no one could ever get angry with your grandmother, no matter what she asked you to do. The title of "Grannie Annie" has stuck with me for all these 24 years.

On another front, Don Day was so unhappy in his new position on the night time weather, that without talking to me first, he had gone up to Mr. Woods' office and quit. (He didn't know that Bob was about to leave WTVY and I couldn't betray Bob's confidence about his decision to move to Montgomery.) All Don had really wanted was to be back on the show with me and do his regular radio work on WTVY- FM.

I was crushed when Don told me what he had done, but his pride kept him from going back to Mr. Woods in order to keep his job. Don worked awhile for WOOF radio before he and his buddy, Sammy Faulk, moved to Montgomery to work at WLWI Radio where they have worked until recently. Don Day has just signed on to go with "Bass Masters."

An added note on Bob Howell: Bob has recently left WSFA to go into upper level management with a large corporation that owns a group of television stations. The Howells still live in Montgomery.

Chapter Four
And then there was Tony Scott

Since Bob Howell and Don Day had left WTVY about the same time, it was necessary to hire someone else to do the show with me. Tony Scott applied and got the job. Here was a brand new challenge for me. I had known Bob and Rex for years before I had actually worked with them . Because I did so much with WTVY-FM, Don Day and I had also become good friends before we started doing the show together. Now, I had to work with a total stranger.

Tony had come directly to us from a rock n' roll radio station and wore his hair very long. He had also been James Brown's road manager at one time. I confess that I was a little apprehensive at first, but I determined that I was going to like this man and work with him just as I had done with my other three co-hosts.

What a pleasant surprise I had with Tony Scott. (His real name is Purvis Lipham.) He was not at all like I had thought he was going to be. Instead, he was one of the sweetest and most genuine men I'd ever known. Was he ever talented, too. He had his own recording studio and could play almost anything on the piano 'by ear".

Tony was a born cut up, and I found myself playing the "straight man" role to his comic behavior. Just to see what I would do, once, Tony and our entire crew all walked out the back door. They even cut the lights off on the camera to make me think we were "off the air". Because I didn't know what else to do, I just kept talking. I definitely spoiled their joke!

...

In 1971, I had been diagnosed with lupus and because of my own battle with this dread disease, I was invited to co-host a benefit for the Lupus Foundation in Atlanta, Ga with WXIA's very popular TV personality, John Wade. This big event was held at the new "Midnight Sun" Dinner Theater with Jack Cassidy starring as Don Quixote in the *Man Of LaMancha*. It was an exciting time for me but my poor husband, Jerome, nearly starved that night because he wouldn't eat the kind of food they served on the elaborate bouffet. As for me, I tried some of everything they served, which included "sushi" (raw fish), rare roast beef , exotic shrimp dishes, wonderful casseroles and elaborate desserts. Jerome ate rolls and water at the dinner, so we hit McDonald's for him after the big show. We did raise a lot of money to assist lupus victims. (Tragically, two weeks after Jack Cassidy's performance in Atlanta, he was burned to death in a hotel fire.)

The next night after the lupus benefit, Jerome and I went to a big area talent show to see the "Country Music Show Case". Tony Scott and I had recently held a country music contest and our local winner was to perform in the regional finals that evening. "Nancy" was a knock out singing "Rocky Top"! Our representative didn't win, but, I was really proud of her. Previously I had asked my friend and childhood classmate, Charlie Monk, who now works in

Nashville, to get a group together and judge the contest for us. His team really did a good job, as was evidenced by Nancy's talented performance.

When I returned from my trip to Atlanta, Tony and I featured a lady with a most interesting career. Heidi Harrell, originally from Galway, Ireland, had finally won the ""World Championship Oyster Shucking Contest" in 1986. She had almost won in 1979, but unfortunately, the judge found one oyster that she had missed. She visited with us right after her win, and performed her "talent" of oyster shucking! We were astonished at her skill and speed. (We also enjoyed the oysters.) Heidi was such a sweet lady and gave God the praise for giving her the ability to "shuck oysters."

The "World's Strongest Man", Paul Anderson, was a gentle giant full of love and compassion. His main purpose in life, he told us, was to help underprivileged children. He was also a true sports role model who gave God all the credit for his remarkable strength.

When I explained to my children how well- behaved and disciplined all the youth were that lived on his ranch, they all said, "Sure they are, Mom, would you misbehave around the world's strongest man?" Good point!

Everyone loves good cooking and one of our most watched segments on our "Morning Show" has been all the great cooks who've demonstrated their ability to cook. After one of these popular programs, we are always flooded with requests for recipes.

Jane Brewer from the Alabama Poultry and Egg Association regularly visited us for years until the Poultry and Egg Association had to cut back on their budget. We were all heartbroken, because not only did Jane bring the greatest dishes, but we loved her as a friend as well. Jane would always prepare a finished product and then put one together on the air. The uncooked one I always took home. My children couldn't wait to sample the latest "Jane Brewer recipe". Our crew got to eat the one that was pre-cooked also.

Jane even taught me how to do crepes, causing my family to go out and purchase a crepe pan. Our sons started making dessert crepes almost every day after this. Steve and Trant loved to experiment with food, but they didn't like to clean up the kitchen!

Nell Jones has been another very popular chef who made regular guest appearances on our show. Her two cookbooks have sold so well that she has virtually sold them all. Nell's specialty is sweet potato soufflé, chocolate cakes and wonderful pies and cookies. Her husband Bill is a great cook in his own right and sometimes he did barbecue recipes for us. Needless to say, the Joneses became an integral part of our WTVY family.

The ladies from Gulf Power in Panama City, Florida, not only shared energy saving tips with us, but they also prepared simple recipes that you can easily do in the microwave. They taught me how to make banana pudding and macaroni and cheese in the microwave. It is a "never fail" method. I also learned how to cook great microwave peanut brittle and other simple dishes. I requested and got, a new microwave oven that Christmas.

Vicki Murphy and Joyce Clanton from the Florida Department of Natural Resources taught us everything you could possibly want to know about cooking fish. Our mailbag was always packed with requests for all of these recipes that we featured. The amount of requests for recipes was a good way to check on who was watching our show. Vicki Murphy's father lived in Dothan, and when she stayed with him, we visited more often. We became great friends and prayer partners.

When one by one, each organization began cutting back on their budgets, it was like losing a member of the family when our guest cooks could no longer come to do our "Morning Show".

After all the time that we had together, it was encouraging to know that God had answered so many prayers on behalf of our chefs. It's wonderful to have good friends who believe in prayer and could also provide great dishes.

...

There was a time when Tony Scott and I went over to do a special at the Vivian B. Adams school in Ozark, Alabama, for retarded students, Jerry Vann had planned to meet us to do the camera work. When he didn't show up, I began to worry, because Jerry is always punctual.

Ray Gene Burkett, the Director of the School, asked one of his students if he knew Jerry Vann. When the young man shook his head and said "Yes.", Mr. Burkett suggested that he walk around to the front of the building to see if Jerry was anywhere outside. After ten or more minutes had passed, when neither Jerry nor the student had showed up, Ray Gene went to look for both of them.

In reality, what had happened was the young boy had done exactly what Mr. Burkett had told him to do, "See if Jerry Vann is outside." In his simple way of thinking, he never deducted that we wanted him to bring Jerry back with him. Jerry later told us that he and the student had been involved in a good long conversation.

(The boy had never once mentioned that we were there.) These students are so very child like. Jerry, had thought we were late because Tony and I had entered the side door near the workshop while Jerry had gone to the front of the school.

...

Tony and I had some rather frightening moments with some very unusual features. In one instance, we had a man on who brought cobra snakes with him. He had already been bitten once by one of his "pets" and had lost the use of part of his hand and arm. We couldn't believe that he was still handling these snakes. While we were talking, one of his snakes got away and slithered under our curtain. The man jumped up to get it with the mike cord still attached to his shirt. He got so tangled up that he turned the basket over and let the rest of the snakes out. We all screamed, called for a break and yelled out for him to "Catch those snakes!" Even after he said he caught them all, we weren't too sure. No one felt safe in the studio for a long, long time.

Everyone enjoyed "Cousin Cliff", a magician from the Alabama Lung Association, who worked with children suffering from asthma. He came on the program to demonstrate how he helped these young people cope with their disease. Cliff really picked on Tony. First, he cut Tony's tie in two, and then failed to put it back together. He had already switched a tie with Tony before the show (but I didn't know this at the time). After this, the two of them teamed up on me. I had no idea that Tony was somewhat of a magician on his own. Tony started doing some of his own tricks and even offered to cut Cliff's tie in half to see if he could do any better than Cliff had in putting it back together. Cliff, rebutted this with "No! That's Okay, Tony".

After "Cousin Cliff's" visit, Tony wanted to do some of his magic every day. Another "trick" Tony pulled off happened when a professional organist visited us. This man offered to teach us how to play the organ in four easy steps. I never could do what he suggested for me to do. Tony (at first) pretended that he couldn't play either, and then, surprisingly , began to play like a "pro". Playing by "ear", Tony did a great "Boogie Woogie". The viewers called all day. They loved it!

"Mr. "Donut" opened in Dothan with Ed Wein the great donut maker. For a programming boost, Tony and I went down to make donuts. I had to pretend to make Tony behave while he went wild making "strange donuts."

It became obvious that Tony and I enjoyed visiting all kinds of restaurants because we loved good food. When the Garland House opened, I went almost immediately to tape a feature. After we ran the interview, those who watched our show flocked in for days to eat at the restaurant. One man insisted on eating a piece of the same pie that I had eaten on the program that day. None of us could remember which kind it was, so Jo Garrett gave him a piece of her chess pie. He said it was wonderful.

In one program, a magician came with a "guillotine". We talked Tony into putting his head in the device and the magician pretended to "cut his head off." It looked very realistic and the man went on and on about how Tony's head was going to fall into the basket. Tony is always a good sport so he acted appropriately nervous. When the magician pulled the cord, the blades came down without Tony suffering any harm, to my relief.

"Mr. Jack", a talking car, was one of our presentations. The Dothan City Police had wired up a blue and white Volkswagen with sound, and headlights that flipped up and down. The car was used to educate children about crime prevention and safety. As I held the mike to interview "Mr. Jack", I heard Tony mumble something behind me. When I turned to ask him what he was saying, he grinned and said, "Don't you feel stupid interviewing a car?"

I bounced back with "No, I don't, it has more intelligence than some people I know!"

Many times Tony and I spotlighted self-defense segments on our show. In the middle of one program Tony pretended to "break his fist" while breaking the boards which our guest had set up. (I never knew when he was serious or teasing.)

Right after we had purchased a very expensive new cyclorama curtain, I invited Mike Sadler and Mike Culbreth to demonstrate the Korean Yoshukai Karate with their weapons. Mike Sadler began his demonstration by breaking a staff across Mike Culbreth's bare chest. The wooden stick splintered and went flying through the air like some sort of out of control "dagger". When it landed, it ripped the new curtain for about two feet! I couldn't believe it! Our crew began to tease me about how long it would take for Mr. Woods to take the cost of the curtain out of my salary. I'm very thankful that Mr. Woods was very understanding, and we got someone to sew it up.

A very tough experience I encountered while doing the program with Tony Scott was the time I completely lost my voice. What started out as simple laryngitis, (I thought at the time) turned into six weeks of total silence on my part. To help correct the problem, I wound up having Dr.

Donald Brice remove a nodule from my vocal cords. A rumor got out that I had throat cancer, and, to alleviate the fears of our friends, we had to do these funny little sketches to let folks know that I was fine except for my voice.

We produced one promo with me moving my lips while Tony talked for me. Another one showed me holding up signs with messages on them. Reading them, Tony would turn to the camera saying, "I thought I'd get to talk a little when she lost her voice, but instead, she writes pages of notes for me to read!" Tony and Teresa Thomas did the show for me during my time of silence, but I continued to do all the planning for it.

When I finally got my voice back, three of Mr. Woods' maiden aunts invited us to visit their farm to do a feature with them. We had a grand time with Miss Kate, Miss Louise and Miss Christine. The ladies were all great cooks in addition to their other talents. There were so many animals there and such beautiful flowers also. Miss Christine had some pet guineas which she could call to come into the barn. We were demonstrating this on camera, when all of a sudden, some of the guineas began chasing Tony. Some ran after him on the ground while others flew over his head. It was not very funny to Tony when it happened, but when Jerry Finn, our production editor, put together the story, it was so humorous.

In the show I'm yelling, "Tony, leave those poor guineas alone!" while he is running around saying, "They're after me! Help! Help!" Jerry put some appropriate chicken clucking music in the background while he alternately made Tony run fast, and then in slow motion throughout the whole program. We got rave reviews! Everywhere we went people expressed how much they enjoyed it.

We also had a lot of fun going to Abbeville, Alabama to meet the Preservation Hall Jazz Band sponsored by the Abbeville Arts Council. My husband, Jerome, is a real jazz buff, and he loved it. Before we knew it, the audience (including us) were dancing in a continuous Congo line. (I was young then.)

Because of Tony's other duties as News and Weather Anchor, I often had to do features on my own. I was invited to go to Montgomery and interview Alabama's First Lady at the time, Cornelia Wallace. We were plugging her new book *Co'nelia,* which was a deliberate misspelling of her name.

Years ago I had briefly attended classes with Cornelia at Huntingdon College in Montgomery. I had always admired her beauty and style. In a short time after we first met, she dropped out of school and hit the road with another friend who helped to back up the country singing stars, the Everly Brothers (Don and Phil), who sang such classics as "Wake Up Little Susie" and "Bye Bye Love", as well as other great hits.

Now, Cornelia was George Wallace's second wife, and she convinced me of her undying love for him. It was a very emotional depiction while Cornelia discussed her memories of the day George Wallace was shot. To my surprise, right after I ran the one hour program, the news broke that she and the Governor were calling it quits! I got a lot of teasing for being so gullible, but that's me! I'd rather think the best of someone than the opposite.

A funny thing that happened during the special with Mrs. George Wallace was what occurred when we aired it again in the early morning hours. (WTVY re-did the program from 2-3:00 a.m. the next morning for those who worked at night. We had a good audience at that time also.)

Anyway, three different women who were in labor while watching the show, decided to name their babies after us. One named her daughter "Cornelia", another mother named her baby girl "Ann" and the third woman had a boy and named him "Tony Scott". When they all called to tell us, we announced the births on the air. (I wonder where those children are today?)

Each year, I have had the privilege of acting as Mistress of Ceremonies for the "Little Miss Dothan" contest, sponsored by the Dothan Pilot Club. One outstanding memory of this event happened when one of the winners appeared on our show after the pageant. When we asked her if she had been nervous that night, she smiled, "No Ma'am! My mother told me to imagine seeing all those judges sitting on the commode when they interviewed me. I did, and I wasn't nervous at all!" Out of the mouths of children!! Her mother was so embarrassed that her daughter had told their "little secret" on the air!

...

Tony Scott and I were often asked to participate in many events outside the TV Station. There was a time when we were invited to ride in a Mardi Gras Parade in Ft. Walton Beach, Florida. Again, Tony's other duties kept him from going, so I had to go alone. It really turned out to be a very unpleasant time for me. How I wished for Tony. We had a big celebrity float with TV personalities from many other stations. The pirate who also rode the float with us was really "wicked looking". My husband was a little hesitant about turning me over to him as the pirate helped me aboard.

In retrospect, the man dressed like a pirate, was the nicest person on the float. Most all of the other TV and radio celebrities were drunk They even began yelling and pelting the crowd with the candy which we had been given to throw to spectators. When I passed Wayne Register with his camera on the side of the street, I realized my new remote microphone was not working. It was probably a good thing, as many in our group were shouting profanities. I couldn't believe it! The pirate kept apologizing for them. I guess I had been so used to the kind of TV personalities we had at WTVY. Our staff would never behave like that! My husband was shocked at what happened, also, and he was sorry that he had misjudged the pirate.

...

Charlie Monk, who grew up with me in Geneva and was now the official "M. C. of Nashville," and I had an invitation to do a benefit for the Association of Retarded Citizens in our hometown. Charlie and some of his "Nashville Cronies" were on our show the morning before the event. With Charlie and Tony Scott, plus the "very odd" young comedian Charlie brought down from the Music City, the show got way out of hand. I tried to get them straightened out, but it was impossible. I really worried that Mr. Woods would be upset but he evidently didn't see the program. Other people who talked to me about the show said they loved it. One never knows what will go over and what won't.

...

Always looking for new and different material, I found out about a newly elected female mayor: I invited her to visit us on the show because she was the first woman we knew of locally who was a Mayor. As she began telling us about her small town, she went on to explain that the new four lane had come through their town causing all the shops and homes to be removed. Tony popped up with, "What? The four lane came through and wiped out your whole town?"

The indignant lady felt insulted at his remark and John Gause, our sales manager, also got upset. Tony had meant no harm, but he always said whatever was on his mind at the moment.

Monkeys do the funniest things. I'll always remember the time a rodeo cowboy and his pet chimp visited us to promote the upcoming rodeo. While Tony was going down to the news set, I began reading our announcements. The cowboy told the monkey to go over and give me a hug.

The chimp came right up and sat down beside me and put his big ol' hairy arm around me. The next thing he did was something that none of us could have predicted. When he saw my necklace, he reached over to get it because he loved "sparkling" things. In doing so, he caused all the pearl buttons on my new silk blouse to come unbuttoned. I had to grab my blouse while the chimp grinned like chimps always do. Immediately, the phone began to ring with viewers complaining that someone had sent the terrible chimp over to insult me. This was certainly not the case. We tried to explain that the monkey really hadn't meant to unbutton my blouse, but Al Klapel, our operations manager, didn't believe this explanation. He even considered canceling the rodeo's commercials because

45

of his distaste for the monkeys stunt. It surely caused a lot of talk in town, and it also proved that our viewers cared about us.

...

For a long time, I had wanted to transfer our 16mm. old home movies to tape, but there was never enough time to do this during the mornings. Since we were now on 24 hours a day, I asked Ernest Williams, one of our production workers, if he could do this for me during one of our midnight movies. "No problem, Ann," he agreed. Two or three nights passed, and he had still not started on the project. I didn't want to rush him, so I had just about forgotten about it.

Ironically, the night Ernest decided to transfer the film for me, my daughter Paige and a friend were spending the night with my sister Paula. Right in the middle of the movie they were watching, the video of my uncle Lamar popped up on the screen. My daughter yelled, "Look, Karen, that looks just like my Granddaddy Jones except he is much thinner." She ran excitedly back to my sister's bedroom to wake her up and tell her what she had seen.

When Paula finally made it back to the den, the WTVY movie was playing again.

"Paige, you must have been dreaming!", Paula mumbled. The two girls declared that they had both seen the same thing. Paula really didn't care at this point what they had seen because she only wanted to go back to bed.

Very shortly after this, Paige really let out a "yelp."

"Look, Karen, that's my Granddaddy Jones. He's wearing his white shirt and pants just like he always did.

That's him! That's him! " When she ran to get Paula this time, Paula was getting very tired of all this nonsense.

"Are you crazy, Paige? Our Daddy's dead! Why are you trying to play a trick on me?," she muttered.

"No, no, I promise, Aunt Paula, come and see him! Maybe it is a sign or something from Heaven that Granddaddy is all right!" Paige said excitedly.

By the time the tired and thoroughly disgusted Aunt Paula got to the TV, the screen was totally blank. She starred at the set until the old WTVY movie came back on again.

This time Paula told the girls that they were never to wake her up again unless the house was on fire, no matter what was on TV.

It was a few days later before I realized what had actually happened. It was the day I found my video tapes and film on my desk. When Ernest came back by my office, I thanked him for all his help and asked him what time he had transferred the film. When I told him what the girls had seen on TV, he really cracked up.

"Oh my Lord, no!" He protested. "I remember now, I fell asleep a couple of times during that movie. I guess that's when your old home movies showed up on the air. I'll bet I'll get in trouble for this."

"No you won't," I laughed, "I'll get you out of it." And, I did. Mr. Woods liked the story, but he told me to warn Ernest "Never to fall asleep on the job again!"

...

Because we at WTVY had become so much like an extended family, there were times when we all got together in the studio to pray about some serious situation in the lives of our co-workers.

When our station owner, Charles Woods, had a blocked aorta and had to undergo emergency surgery, we all gathered together and earnestly prayed for him. He did have a very speedy recovery, and he gave credit to God for seeing him through it. On another occasion, our station manager, Betty Griffin, discovered a lump in her breast. She was really nervous, and as I prayed with her over the phone, it was very evident that she was getting emotional. Amazingly, the lump was benign, and again, we knew that God had answered our prayers.

Judy Kirkland, who worked in traffic with Reggie Mitchell was told that she had to have a kidney transplant. Not only was she very upset, but she feared she wouldn't be able to get one in time. To express our love and concern, we all got together and prayed for Judy. Thankfully, God was merciful to her. Eventually, Judy did have to get a second kidney transplant but she is doing wonderfully well today!

James Robison had been to Dothan many times and during one of his one night meetings at the Dothan Civic Center, he brought Sam Mings, a fellow co-worker with him. That night each of these men shared that both of them had almost been "aborted" had not God intervened.

This was a very unusual set of events because only that very afternoon, before coming to James's meeting, I had overheard a conversation about one of our co-workers who had just discovered that she was pregnant. This lovely young lady was a Christian who already had one daughter when her husband had just walked out on her. Because he had left her for another woman and had simply "disappeared", this distraught young woman had decided to have an abortion.

I was so heartbroken about this that I knew I had to try to do something to stop it, but I didn't know what to do.

That night after the meeting, my husband and I talked this over with James and Sam. We decided to join forces in prayer for God to show me what I needed to do to somehow stop my friend from aborting her baby. After we prayed, Sam Mings spoke up and insisted that after I had a chance to talk with this young lady that I should call him at his motel room at their next stop, in order for him to share with her also.

I was so concerned about this sweet lady that I prayed every time I woke up that night. The next morning I got to the station very early and left a note on her desk which simply read, "I love you _____, and whatever you decide to do, I will always love you, but please come by my office when you get in."

It was time for the "Morning Show", so Tony and I got ready. I had no choice but to press on through, "Sunny Side Up!" The program was over before the lump in my throat came back. No sooner had I made it back to my office when this young woman came in right behind me. I did what seemed the natural thing to do, I hugged her and held her for a few moments like a mother would hold her child, and then, I asked her to sit down.

I honestly don't remember what I said to her, but I did ask her if she would please talk with my friend Sam Mings before she made her final decision concerning her baby. She nodded her agreement. In a few minutes, I had Sam Mings on the phone. He had arrived at his destination only a few hours before and he was still very sleepy. It was difficult for him to think, much less talk. Sam asked for a few minutes to wash his face and wake up. It seemed like an eternity before he came back to the phone. When he did, I handed her the phone and said, "Meet Sam Mings." I don't know to this day what he said to her but I imagine part of it was the events of his life which he had told us about the night before at the Dothan Civic Center.

Sam Mings told us this story: Sam's mother was a very young girl the night she went on a date with a boy she hardly knew. He put something in her soft drink (as I remember) and knocked her out. She came to at her doorsteps. She had no idea what had happened to her. In due time after missing two of her periods, she finally told her mother. A local doctor confirmed what they suspected.

"Your daughter is eight weeks pregnant," he told the weeping pair. "We can't do abortions legally in this state, but there is a little clinic right over the state line that may can help you." he added. He gave the young girl's mother the phone number of the clinic.

The exact facts after this are blurred, but, for some reason, the family decided not to terminate the pregnancy, and so, little Sam was born. In those days, most babies born "out of wedlock" were looked down on and their mothers were put to shame. In this case, by contrast, not only did Sam's mother's family lovingly support her, but the entire church she attended did so also. Her very wise and Godly pastor prayed for God to send just the right father for little Sam. Two and a half years later, Sam's mother married a wonderful Christian man who adopted Sam and raised him as his own.

Whether Sam Mings told her this story or not, I don't know, whatever he did tell her worked.. Her face changed from coldness to tears. She hurriedly handed me back the phone.

"I can't do this, I can't. I can't kill my baby!" she cried.

All I had time to say to Sam was "Thanks Sam, keep on praying. I'll stay in touch."

The next thing out of her mouth, as, again, I held her in my arms was, "What am I going to do? I don't have insurance and I don't have any money."

Just then I looked down at my desk. The scripture of the day on my prayer calendar read: "Come boldly to the throne of Grace, to find help in time of need." So, I said, "Oh that's easy! We'll ask the Father what to do." As we were praying, my phone rang. The person on the other end is very wealthy and loves children. I told him what had just happened, and without hesitation, he told me to tell her not to worry about a thing that he would pay for her baby. She was overwhelmed.

On the very day she had previously scheduled to go to a clinic in Montgomery to have an abortion, she was at my Ob-Gyn's office getting her first check up. Dr. Clyde Smith was as loving and supportive of her as he possibly could be, The girls at WTVY pitched in, helped her get maternity clothes, and gave her a shower for the new baby.

We all went to see her in the hospital when her second little daughter was born. (All the men, too). She never felt isolated or alone. From the earliest days, it was obvious that this baby was very special. She rarely ever cried and had the sweetest spirit about her. As the little girl grew up, she always tried to please her mother and was the peacemaker in the family. Although this young lady and her girls have moved to another city, when they do visit us, the second-born daughter always runs to me and hugs me over and over. She has never been told what almost happened to her, but just the same, she knows, as I do, that there is a special bond between us.

...

Tony Scott and I have been able to meet some very outstanding foreigners who were religious leaders in their own countries. One man, Dr. Albert Hibbert, from England, had grown up in the shadow of Smith Wigglesworth, the great man of God who could never read a word until after his conversion to Christ, and after this experience, he could read the Bible perfectly, (But nothing else.)

On and on Rev. Hibbert went, as he described the miracles he saw in the ministry of Smith Wigglesworth. Soon, he began to tell us about the end times and what he believed would happen shortly before the end. After the show was over, Tony was still talking with him. (In those days, we could have one guest on for an entire show if we chose to do so.)

Subsequently, we met Don O'Don, also from England. Tony listened to all he had to say about what God was doing all over the world. This great man of faith believed nothing was impossible with God.

Tony had met James Robison and the lovable John McKay, who was the singer for James's crusades. He listened intently as they shared their own stories. Bible teacher Dudley Hall made regular visits to our program bringing his special gift of making Biblical truths practical in day to day life. There were others, too. Some of our guests were precious little senior citizens who always thanked God for their blessings, and even, a few gifted artists, who said that God had given them their talent.

There was no doubt that Tony knew where I stood concerning the things of the Lord. It was not surprising, then, that during one of the hardest times in Tony's life, he showed up at our door one night. Jerome and I spent hours talking to him, and soon after, Tony went to his father's farm in North Alabama. He found a quiet spot, knelt in the middle of those woods and surrendered everything to God. He has been a different person ever since.

Chapter Five
Tough on the outside, a softy at heart - Chris Bence

Mr. Woods had made up his mind. He wanted Tony Scott to do both the six o'clock and ten o'clock weather. Tony couldn't work both the morning and the night time slots, on that account, Chris Bence, the new manager of WTVY - FM was given the job of being my new co-host. Even though Tony was, at the time, deeply disappointed; therefore, I did everything I could do to encourage him.

It was evident that Chris must be thinking that I was going to resent his coming to do the program with me, because he had often observed me trying to console Tony. To clear matters up, I decided to call him and set up an appointment.

Chris was a little surprised that I wanted to talk with him, and, I guess, a little leery of my motives. I assured him that even though I dearly loved and appreciated Tony, that I was willing to work with him in every way. He still looked suspicious of me as I left his office, but I knew I had done exactly what I was supposed to do.

To tell the truth, Chris Bence was my hardest case. Looking back, all of my co-hosts had entirely different levels of involvement in regards to the program. Rex Roach had bubbled with knowledge and had a very inquisitive nature, but he had not wanted to do any of the planning or programming for our show. I had to do it all. He still did an excellent job as an interviewer because he knew something about almost everything.

Bob Howell was so thoroughly involved that he not only helped me with all the interviews, (even the cooking segments), but he assisted in planning the show, wrote many of our spots, and spent hours helping me grow and develop.

Don Day was a total opposite from Bob. He could care less about planning for anything. He had a true D. J.' s heart and loved to wing it! He enjoyed the show so very much that to him the work was never serious but just a fun way to relate to people. Most of the time, he would even forget what question he had previously asked. Rex and Bob had been like "big" brothers. Don Day was more like my son. Our viewers, had totally accepted and loved all three. Their very different personalities were still appealing to all ages.

Tony Scott had been my clown and my alter ego. I always played the straight man (like Bud Abbott) to his comic ways (like Lou Costello). It was hard to keep a straight face with Tony around. (To tell on him, he had even tried to tip Santa Claus over in his chair when Santa made his annual visit to us.) Tony never wanted to plan for the show, except, occasionally when he would suggest some guest or topic of interest.

When Chris joined me, I saw the same motivation that I had seen in Bob Howell, plus the sexy good looks of Don Day. Chris was very serious and was determined to change our program to make it the best ever. I knew that he felt I would resist his ideas in every way. That's why I told him what I really felt in my heart:

"Chris, I am old fashioned, and I believe that the man should always be the leader. This is not my show, it is now our show. Anything you want to do differently, we'll try."

It was obvious that he didn't believe me. The first thing he did was change our theme music. After listening to it, I really liked it and when the viewers heard it, they liked it as well. Chris chose a theme song based on a medley by Lou Christy including "Good Morning" and "Zip A Dee Doo Dah!" We started getting requests for the music, but it was no longer available to sell.

To continue Chris's new ideas, our very talented videographer, Bobby "Red" Flournoy, shot some brand new scenes for us which included coffee bubbling in the pot, a farmer driving a tractor at sun-up, some children swinging in the yard and other down home scenes. The phone rang and rang as our viewers expressed their approval.

Very soon, I sensed that Chris always wanted to come across as very knowledgeable and professional. I committed to help him achieve his goal of looking good in every situation. I fixed his coffee, placed his script right beside him and marked the things that he needed to know. He was honestly not prepared for the way I treated him. Every other TV personality he had ever met had always given him a hard time. I think he expected me to get angry at any time if I didn't like something he did.

Then, suddenly, the change came. One morning as we were preparing for our opening billboard, he leaned over and pointed to his script. "This name is wrong!", he said.

As I did all the typing I guess he thought I had made a mistake. I quickly told him the name was correct. "Her name is Teretha Federick!"

"You mean Teresa Frederick, don't You?" he asked.

By this time, we were almost at the point of appearing on camera. "No, I whispered, I know her real well, her name is Teretha Federick!" Then we were on.

In his very best radio style deep voice, he opened the show with his usual "Good Morning" to our viewers and to me. It was my turn to preview the show. Next, he was to introduce our first guest, and he did. In his most professional voice, he announced, "Our first guest this morning is Teretha Federick from the Houk- Hoston Boys Club...I mean the Hos..." he paused, he couldn't say it! He had concentrated so hard on her name and never making a mistake that somewhere along the way he lost it. I reached over, patted his knee and sympathized with him by explaining, "Bless your heart, Chris, you've been hanging around with me too much. It's the Hawk- Houston Boys Club."

He smiled, and we continued with the interview. How could something that simple change everything? I don't know, but it did.

Maybe he stopped taking himself so seriously, or perhaps, he started trusting in me a little.

It was not long before Chris and I had the kind of bonding I had experienced with his predecessors. Bob, Don and Chris, more than any of the others, insisted on calling me "Grannie Annie". Often, Chris would slip up and call me this on the air. We got a lot of calls on why he did this. I had to explain that it was not an insult but a compliment.

Because Chris was so committed to stay involved with all aspects of our show, he enjoyed accompanying me on our out of town trips. On one such trip, when we did a special together at Panama City Beach, Buddy Wilkes, Director of the Miracle Strip Amusement Park, pulled a really mean trick on us. Right after we had finished a huge meal at the Treasure Ship, Buddy invited us to ride one of his new rides. He promised that we would only go around once for the camera. So, because we trusted him, we loaded up our families and climbed aboard. He lied! Instead, he wouldn't let the ride operator stop. We begged and pleaded but he just laughed and laughed.

My poor husband was sitting down toward the inside while I was forced by the pull of gravity to lie over on him. He got sicker and sicker until he threw up! We promised Buddy we would get even!

When at last, he allowed us to stop, he was so apologetic and begged us to forgive him. He assured us that he had no idea we were getting so sick. Jerome had to leave and return to our motel room.

Buddy asked me for one more favor. He promised he would behave and would even ride with us if Chris and I would just get on the swings for a brief ride. Again, trusting Buddy, we climbed aboard. Chris was in front, and I was in the middle of the two of them. Wayne Register started up the camera. It was a nightmare! Buddy began turning and twisting my swing and Chris could do nothing to help. He was already nauseated himself, and it took all he could do to keep his WTVY- FM cap on his head. Wayne and Chris both threatened Buddy if he didn't stop. It was a long time before he did, nevertheless.

Perhaps Buddy didn't realize how very sick we were, but whatever the case, we promised him we would seek vengence no matter what. Even Wayne Register got sick later that night because Buddy had taken him through the "Abominable Snowman" showcase in order to video tape some scenes . It had rocked and rolled until Wayne lost his equilibrium and became ill. We all went to bed that night very uncomfortable.

We, at last, did pay Buddy back. Here's what happened:

Our crew was taping a segment with a very nervous lady out on a local pier when Buddy, up to his usual tricks, began to tickle her legs in an effort to make her even more agitated. That did it! Right in the middle of the interview I pointed to Wayne Register who had the camera on us, "Just look, Wayne, what in the world do you think that crazy Buddy Wilkes is up to now?" Wayne, following my lead, moved the camera down to Buddy. We refused to edit the tape!

Buddy turned as red as a beet because he couldn't believe we did that on camera! Monday when Chris and I returned to do the show, Chris added his own revenge by telling our viewers how much we had enjoyed the week-end with Buddy Wilkes and Susan. (That was not Buddy's wife's name.) From then on, after we taught him a lesson, Buddy has been a straight arrow with us. He really is a wonderful guy!

...

It was in the midst of a terrible electrical storm in Dothan that some power poles fell down near Jerry Vann's house. Jerry's wife, Barbara, called the city to report the wires being down, but people in the electrical department assured her that they were all dead wires by then.

Unfortunately, that was not true, because shortly after this, Jerry's young son and a friend decided to play Tarzan and swing on the wires over a gully. As Chip touched the wires, he was electrocuted. The shock burned part of his left hand and sparks flew out through his tennis shoes. Eventually, he lost his left ring finger and damaged his middle finger on that hand. His left great toe is gone plus he lost two toes on his right foot. How he survived no one knows.

All of us at WTVY were grieved by the terrible tragedy. As we gathered around the Vanns to offer our love and support, we felt again the family closeness of the WTVY staff. I carried Chip a "Kermit" the frog doll who would "take" all his shots for him. Jerry and Barbara took Chip to a special hand surgeon in New Orleans who did everything he could to help Chip. Much prayer went up on Chip's behalf.

Although Chip suffered severe injuries, he has grown up to be a remarkable young man who not only excelled in sports but had all the friends and girlfriends one could possibly have. He is still very close to all of us at WTVY.

...

Carrie Deloney came to work with us right out of college. Jerry Vann hired her as a reporter. Whenever he got tough on Carrie, Chris and I took up for her because she was one of the sweetest and purest girls we had ever known. She was a regular attendee of the singles department at First Baptist Church that Jerome and I directed.

Once Jerry sent Carrie to cover a story about a rapist. (He was the army officer who broke in on couples, raped the women while he held a gun on the man.) Finally, he was apprehended. The court date was set for his trial and our news department was covering the story. For some reason, Carrie got nervous when she saw this man. To protect herself, she hid behind one of the columns in the courthouse while she tried to tape the story. The feature turned out poorly, and she got into trouble over this. Chris and I rushed to her aid by scolding Jerry for sending someone like Carrie to do this terrible story.

Jerry just threw up his hands, "She's supposed to do news, Ann, not just fluff stories!" Because he loved Carrie as well, she got away with a lot.

Late one afternoon, Carrie called me at home. "I've just got to meet Dallas Holm!", she excitedly said. "Can you go down to the Civic Center with me about 5:30 and do a story with me?" Of course, for Carrie, I agreed.

At 5:30 I was there, and so was the author of the newest Christian hit single "Rise Again", Dallas Holm, but Carrie Deloney was no where in sight. Fifteen minutes later, while I tried to occupy Mr. Holm's time, Carrie came bouncing out of the bathroom. She had been primping!

The interview was a total success, but when Carrie discovered that he had recently married, she seemed to lose all interest. It was almost time for his band to warm up when we finished, and said our good-byes. Carrie packed up her equipment to head for another assignment. I went home.

The next day I expected to find the interview on my desk. When it was not there, I questioned Carrie. Carrie grabbed her head. "Oh no! I forgot about the interview. I taped over it!" That was the last of that. No one ever got to see Dallas Holm on the "Morning Show."

Today Carrie is married to attorney Keith Givens, has two fine sons and still lives in Dothan where she is a full time homemaker.

...

I got an alarming call early one Saturday morning. Jason Bence, Chris's young son was critically ill with some kind of bacterial infection that the doctors could not isolate. I quickly dressed to go be with Chris. It was obvious that this was no ordinary problem so powerful prayer was needed. As I hugged Chris and his wife, I assured them that only God had the answers to this. It was a touch and go situation with Jason that lasted quite a few days, but each time we faced a serious concern, there was a breakthrough. Jason got a "Kermit the Frog" doll, just like Chip's, to "take" all his shots.

At last when Jason was out of danger, we all felt God's assurance of His blessings. I knew, then, that Chris was really on his way to trusting God for everything in his life.

...

When it was time again to go the CBS Star weekend, Chris packed his cowboy hat and boots so he could hang in there with the likes of Gerald McCraney and Tom Selleck. We were both excited at the line up of CBS stars that we were to meet.

Soon after we got to our hotel, Chris and I spotted Tom Selleck in the lunch line. Everyone in the entire room was all staring at him. He was wearing a red checked shirt with a white collar, light blue faded jeans, white tennis shoes and no socks. He was probably the most handsome human being I had ever seen. Men and women alike were all in awe of this new TV star. Lucky us, Chris and I were in line right behind him. I even managed to engage him in conversation. He was so easy to talk to in spite of his new star status!

A strange thing happened when Tom Selleck came to our suite for the interview about his show *Magnum P. I.* Tom was so youthful and funny that he reminded me of my two sons Trant and Steve. He had a very contagious little boy laugh. We even found out that he had never smoked in his life in spite of the deceptive "Winchester" cigarette ad that had helped start his career.

"I only made $100 for that ad." he confessed. "I shudder to think that I probably helped encourage people - maybe even kids - to smoke. I'll never do anything that dumb again."

After Tom Selleck's interview, Parker Stevenson and his TV brother, Gerald McCraney of *Simon and Simon* came in. That was it! Whatever Gerald McCraney had was pure animal magnetism. No, he wasn't as physically handsome as Tom Selleck. True, he was balding, while Tom's hair was lush and full, but never had I met a star before (not even Robert Wagner) who caused me to feel like a teenage fan! I even messed up the interview at the beginning. Chris was amused! The younger women were all excited about Parker Stevenson , but I'm totally sold on Gerald McCraney.

By reason of the fact that both Chris and I are somewhat conservative in our politics, we were very impressed that both Tom Selleck and Gerald McCraney also shared our same political views.

Gerald McCraney has really continued to prove himself as an actor. When he married Delta Burke, I think that was a prefect match. The fact that he still loves her even after she has gained weight, shows what a good man he is. I hope I'll always think this well of him.

Brooke Sorrell came rushing into our suite all dressed in white as "Boss Hogg", the feisty character on *The Dukes of Hazzard.* We enjoyed his funny mannerisms so very much even when he demanded that we refer to him in no other way but "Boss Hogg!" He really did cause us to become a little curious by insisting later that he needed to change clothes. When he came out of our bathroom, he had on a dark jacket.

"Now," he explained, "I am Brooke Sorrell. You may interview me now!" That was just another quirk we discovered about TV stars.

Gordon Jump, the TV manager of the imaginary radio station *WKRP in Cincinnati,* did a wonderful interview with us. Since he and Chris had both worked in radio, they really enjoyed comparing how true to life some of the happenings seen on the television show were compared to what did happen in the real world of radio. (Today, Gordon Jump is the actor who portrays the Maytag repairman.)

Chris talked me into something that year that turned out rather well. All the kitchen help, hotel maids, bellboys, and other general workers would stand in line outside our taping suites for a chance to get an autograph from one of the CBS celebrities. The stars, themselves, were on such a tight schedule that they never had time to grant their requests. One afternoon, I opened the door to see if our next CBS star was outside since he was already late for our next interview. When all the help spotted me standing there, they ran up to me to beg for my autograph. I tried in vain to explain to them that I wasn't a CBS star but just a local TV talk show hostess. They were still clamoring over me when somehow, I managed to squeeze back inside the room.

Chris asked why all the commotion and when I explained, he grinned, "Grannie, in that Hollywood looking animal print blouse you have on, you look like a star! Go ahead and do it! What could it hurt?"

"Chris," I answered back, "That would be wrong! Those people think I'm somebody."

"You are," he said. "You're Ann Varnum. They didn't ask who you were, they just asked for an autograph."

So, he pushed me out the door, and I wrote my name until I had writer's cramp. All of the workers smiled with pleasure. At last, I had signed every one of the requests. When I looked up, our next guest had arrived. I still don't remember who it was, but I think it was one of those soap opera stars.

Anyway, after we finished for the day, I went down to the CBS media room and picked up stacks of autographed CBS star pictures. The CBS folks looked at me a little suspiciously because those postcard sized prints had previously been passed out to those of us who were with affiliate stations. I just went right ahead with my mission as if this were a perfectly normal thing to do.

Did I ever have fun giving out all those pictures. I even went into the big hotel kitchen and gave the kitchen help autographed prints. They were all so thrilled. Some workers attempted to kiss my hand! Many could not speak English, but they shook their heads in gratitude. Their smiles were worth all my efforts.

What happened later that night was beyond what I could have imagined. It was "dress up" night and all the big CBS executives, the biggest stars and the affiliate stations' representatives were being treated to a very special dinner and presentation. Obviously, I wanted to look my best, so I told the men to go on down, and I would join them later. I needed to finish my last minute "touch ups."

When I walked into that huge ballroom, there were ice sculptures and the most elegant food I had ever seen on large tables. The room was filled with celebrities of every kind, from the big name stars to the CBS executives. The lights were dimmed, so I had to look very hard for our WTVY crew. Just as I got three or four feet inside the door, I heard an excited voice saying, "Right this way, please ma'am!" Taking me by the arm, a waiter began escorting me to the number one table in the room.

"No, no," I protested. "I have to sit with my friends. They're here somewhere."

It was no use! He sat me at the big round table with all these "big name" stars and studio executives. I also sat in the last available seat there, as if it had been saved for me.

Then, to my further astonishment, I was surrounded by waiters trying to give me wine (I don't drink) or tea or coffee. They brought me a flower that one of the little waitresses had fixed for me. All at once, it began to dawn on me what was happening. Either they all thought that I really was a big name star, or they wanted to show their appreciation to me. Whatever the case, I was treated royally all night. I never had to ask for anything. They even brought me the dessert tray twice.

I know the table full of celebrities wondered who I was also. When I finally explained to them why I believed I was being treated so special, they all seemed to enjoy the story immensely. In fact, the rest of the week-end, many of the stars even came and sat with our TV crew at mealtime; since, we always seemed to receive preferred treatment. (I have always wondered if those workers tried to find "Ann Varnum" on the CBS shows!)

...

A very dear couple visited "The Morning Show" to share the incredible story of their ministry. Clift Brannon had been the personal attorney of R. G. LeTourneau, the inventor and developer of the huge earth moving machines. Mr. LeTourneau was so wealthy that he gave ninety percent of his income to the Lord and lived off the ten percent. Clift had traveled many miles with this unusual man sharing in his desire to spread the Gospel.

The two men gave away bibles that had been pre-marked with explicit directions to help someone understand the plan of salvation. Clift's wife, Ruth, had initially fought this whole "religious" fervor. She even threatened to leave Clift if he insisted on pursuing this "wholesale evangelism ministry."

"I married an attorney," Ruth stated, "not a preacher. Clift was going to walk away from his career to pursue what I considered , at the time, to be ridiculous."

Cliff Brannon had continuously prayed two prayers: "God, please heal my young daughter, Madeline, and save my wife Ruth!" The Brannons had a beautiful child who was dying of a condition which caused an abnormal growth in her breast bone. This ailment would one day destroy her lungs and other organs. In His mercy, God intervened and answered Cliff's prayers.

Circumstances became worse before they changed, and there came a day when and angry Ruth started packing her bags to leave Clift. All of a sudden, their maid began yelling her name, "Miss Ruth, Miss Ruth, come here!"

When Ruth Brannon entered the room of her child Madeline, she gasped. There lay her tiny daughter breathing perfectly normal. The protruding breast bone was gone! Ruth knelt in amazement beside her child's bed. The affliction the doctors had said would eventually kill Madeline by snuffing out her breath as the deformed breast bone grew had simply disappeared. The scripture that came to Ruth's mind right then was "In my Father's house are many mansions!" It was not your usual salvation passage, but it was all that was needed. By the time Clift arrived home, he had a new wife and a well daughter.

Ruth went on to further explain, "I had always wanted pretty clothes and nice things. I thought I could always have them because Clift was a very successful lawyer. I finally came to realize if God has already prepared a mansion for me in Heaven and had miraculously healed my child, why couldn't I trust Him with every aspect of my life? That was my big turn around."

Today, Madeline has one of the most beautiful singing voices I have ever heard. In fact, until two years ago, when Clift developed some heart problems, the entire family were in ministry together giving away bibles and teaching others how to share the message of Christ.

While he was in Dothan, Clift insisted on giving Chris and me some bibles to use in any way that we saw fit. He even gave me some Spanish New Testaments. (But, that's another story.)

...

Another favorite memory that I shared with Chris Bence was the visit of a tiger cub from Lion Country Safari near Atlanta. We had just acquired a new set for our show, and when the little fellow began clawing the couch, I picked him up. Could he hiss! I turned him over and began rubbing his tummy like I do my cats.

"No, no," the handler exclaimed. "That's what mama tigers do to encourage her cubs to go to the bathroom!"

The look on Chris's face was priceless! Immediately, I put him down.

...

Jeremiah Denton was campaigning for U. S. Senator. I had seen the movie about the awful things he and fellow Vietnam prisoners of war had endured at the hands of the communists. I cried all through the movie and knew that I would always love this wonderful man. When I got a chance to interview him, I was the one who was honored.

It was such a good interview because I know that this man believed everything he was saying. His eyes were really red from late night travel, so, before he left, I put some of my eye drops (for allergies) in his eyes and gave him the rest of the bottle.

I later got a nice thank you note for the interview and a request for more eye drops-ha! Senator Denton won his first election but he didn't know much about politics and campaigning. For that reason, he failed to be re-elected for a second term. Afterwards, I interviewed his wife and heard the whole story from her lips about the start of the POW-MIA program which she and other wives had started in order to wake up our government to the plight of the missing soldiers still imprisoned in Vietnam. Had their effort failed, Jeremiah Denton and others like him would have died in prison.

...

Mr. Howard Hobart was in his 90's when he began visiting our "Morning Show". He had wonderful stories to tell and would bring us muffins, cinnamon bread or some other special treat. We often went to his house to eat lunch because he insisted on feeding us. Chris and I really learned to love this man. Every year on his birthday, we gave him a big birthday party during our show.

My husband, Jerome, and I would often stop by to visit this innovative old man. On one such visit, he told Jerome that he'd better be good to me, or I could come live with him! Jerome started calling him my "93 year old boyfriend". Once, Mr. Hobart shared a story that he experienced as a child. As he told us what he had seen, there was no doubt that it had actually happened.

"My mother died when I was a young boy," he explained, "and I missed her very much. One Sunday my father and I left for church real early so that he could start the stove for the church to get warm before folks arrived. As we stood together at the church door, we turned around and looked up in the sky. It was like a zipper unzipping Heaven, and we saw a beautiful, huge creature all dressed in the most beautiful blue apparel just looking down at us. It was the most wonderful thing I had ever seen. Then, it was gone. When I asked my father what it was, he said, 'One of God's angels, son!' "We never mentioned it again." Mr. Hobart finished.

I told him I believed it was God's way of comforting him over the death of his mother. Mr. Hobart had only told this story to a few people for fear they would laugh at him. Jerome and I surely didn't laugh. I believed in Mr. Hobart's experience so much that I shared his angel story with Nita Hogg when she was a news correspondent for the *Birmingham News*. Nita included it in her series on angels. Mr. Hobart was so thrilled over this.

When Howard Hobart died, his pastor, Dr. Jack Noble of Northside Methodist Church included Mr. Hobart's angel story at his funeral. Jack Noble certainly believed it was true.

Mr. Hobart's granddaughter, Maureen Quale is presently my husband's secretary at Southern Engineered Products. We talk about Mr. Hobart often.

...

A rodeo was coming to town, and for that reason, the rodeo promoter challenged me to ride in on a buffalo to promote the big event. I wasn't nervous about riding the buffalo, but, it was the cowboy I didn't trust. He was much too personal. Chris saw the look in my eyes and came to my rescue. I'm not too sure either that the cowboy wasn't a little tipsy that morning. Anyway, by my riding into the studio on the buffalo we got a lot of attention from our viewers. My mother was greatly alarmed over this even after the fact. I was reminded how many arms, legs, and other parts I could have broken. (That's mothers for you.)

...

Mrs. Eleanor Fiorella was our delightful Mrs. Santa Claus. Year after year until her death, she always visited us near Christmas time passing our her goodies and telling

Christmas stories to the boys and girls. Our WTVY employees were part of her family. She was another regular guest on our show.

Pistol Pete's real name was Arthur Ritchie. He was a pioneer type man who did unusual art using barnyard artifacts. He had a "mail order bride" for awhile until he decided the single life was better and sent her back. He entered every art contest we had. One of his favorite themes was Indian folklore. He had just completed a huge Indian head made of plaster craft to present to us. When poor Chris picked it up, it literally fell apart and slid off the plaque. Chris looked at me and I looked at him.

"Well," he groaned, "you win some, you lose some!" Chris had definitely learned to "hang loose" and not take matters so seriously.

...

Another favorite guest of ours was Mrs. Florence Hodges who was a dedicated volunteer at the South Alabama Medical Center even late into her 90's. She had a marvelous sense of humor and was invited to appear on *The Johnny Carson Show*. She really cracked Johnny up when she told of the phone call she had received from President George Bush to congratulate her on being a "point of light".

"I was on the toilet when he called me, and I didn't even believe he was who he said he was at first", she giggled. "Later, when I realized he was the President, I was so embarrassed."

Mrs. Hodges also made sure Johnny knew who her friends were and who provided her wardrobe. She is one lady who will be greatly missed in our town.

...

When Governor Fob James fulfilled a promise to me by returning to do our "Morning Show" after his election, his media representative had just resigned. After visiting with Chris and me for the show, (we had breakfast for him and everything) he went back to the motel where he had spent the night. Later that day when I got a phone call from him asking me to tell him more about Chris, I knew I wasn't going to like what was about to happen. The rest is history. Chris went to work for Fob James in Montgomery, even though he was still able to oversee WTVY- FM. What he couldn't do, however, was co-host the "Morning Show" with me.

I sighed, "God, I love these men so much. They are all like my brothers. Just when we have developed a wonderful relationship with all the kinks worked out, they leave me!"

"Grannie, I love you and I'll miss you. I won't be far away." Chris said, and then he was gone.

Then, back came Tony Scott to do the show with me again.

Chapter Six
And back comes Tony Scott

"Peep Peep" was a pet quail. He had been raised from an egg by an old gentleman from the panhandle of Florida. It was really remarkable how much the little quail reacted to his master as if it thought that this man was it's parent. "Peep Peep" made several guest appearances on the show and often did what birds are supposed to do, on our coffee table! Nevertheless, Tony and I enjoyed watching the little bird play with his toys and do tricks. Our audience loved "Peep Peep", and some viewers even wrote to him.

...

In the mail one day, we got a most interesting letter and video tape from a man who told us that his pet poodles could actually "play the piano." It did appear (at least on the video) that they were actually playing, so we said, "Why not?" and invited them up for the show.

It was a disaster. Their poor owner was so excited that he didn't consider that having them in a new place might confuse them. First, he couldn't get them to stay on the piano seat. Next, they heard some other dogs in the back who were scheduled for our "Pet of the Week" segment, and they went crazy barking! Our time was running out causing the owner to began begging them, "Please, play the piano for Miss Ann! Please come on now, be good doggies, play for Miss Ann."

By this time, I seriously doubted they ever would perform, but I felt so sorry for the distraught man that I gave them every chance. Tony and the cameramen had already almost collapsed from laughing so hard, while I tried to give them all the "evil eye" to try to make them straighten up.

When the time was up, I began to explain that we'd have them back on again when they weren't so nervous. Even then, their master insisted that they could do other tricks and began having them push little cars and tricycles. The next thing that happened the man started hyperventilating, and we had to pull the plug. It was way past our commercial time and Joe Earl Holloway, our director, was yelling at us to call for a break. That segment was talked about for weeks.

...

Medical news has always been very important to our viewers. To capitalize on this, I began hosting "A Visit with your Doctor" on Fridays. Our topics ran the gamut from heart disease, obesity, female problems, cancer, and even new treatment modalities to encourage overall wellness. Our ratings for these segments were always excellent. Call-ins were also a regular part of these medical shows. That first year that we started the new format, I was honored to receive the Douglas Cannon Award for medical reporting. I'm sure Dr. Rufus Lee and Dr. William Shelor had a lot to do with my nomination.

...

Robert and Frances Woodall had become good friends with Tom Lester who for years had portrayed the character of "Eb" on the TV show *Green Acres* . I had a chance to interview Tom in the Woodall home. We learned all about "Arnold the pig", among other things.

Tom reminded us that pigs are very intelligent, would perform only for treats and would "balk" whenever they wanted to do so. That's why there were a number of "Arnolds" in the show, and since pigs grow so fast, a new bunch (trained, of course) had to be brought in periodically. Much to my relief, Tom also told us that none of the pigs were eaten. Instead, all the "Arnolds" were given a wonderful life on a farm where they remained "pets" much like our cats and dogs.

Tom Lester is a very dedicated Christian who travels around the country today as an inspirational speaker. Next to his love for God, Tom loves fishing and hunting, especially with ol' pal Robert Woodall.

In Chris's absence, Tony Scott was now helping out at WTVY- FM. Because he was also doing weather and news at night, he was not always able to do interviews or go on location with me.

...

Panama City Beach, Florida, has always been the second home for many of our area residents, so we expanded our show by carrying it to Panama City. We covered the Indian Summer Seafood Festival with founder Aaron Besant even before the Panama City stations did.

Our local sales representative Gina Covert made sure we had excellent features to cover while we were there.

Panama City Beach Police Chief Lee Sullivan was always available for a guest appearance. When he visited with us, we usually discussed safety efforts on the beaches. One year, I invited the "Petticoat Junction" gunfighters to join us out by the water while Lee was on our show. Well, they ran on with their stage pistols a'blazing which almost caused Lee's heart to stop! What I had not been told until later was that Lee Sullivan's life had recently been threatened.

"Lady," Lee stammered, "You have scared the wits out of me!" When he told me about the threats, I was so sorry for what had happened.

"No harm done," he assured me. "I'll just have to take it easy the rest of the day."

On another trip to the beach, Bobby "Red" Flournoy was traveling with me to tape a feature on Gulf World. "Red" wanted to make sure he got some good shots of their newest exotic birds, so we asked the lady "bird" handler to take the birds out of their cages. As she was moving one of the new birds, he flew away. For some reason his wings had not been properly clipped; therefore, he could still fly. Well, we all piled into the station car and began the "bird chase". We lost sight of him many times, and by then, I was really praying hard. At last, the frightened bird was caught and returned to Gulf World. We decided not to tape any more birds that trip.

That was the trip that I went up to the dive tanks at Gulf World with the dolphin trainer to help do the show. The female dolphin kept spraying water on me. It seems that dolphins "sense" the sex of a person and this one only liked men. By the time the act was over, I was sopping wet! The audience really enjoyed this particular show and applauded accordingly.

We made so many good friends at Panama City Beach and the food there is wonderful! Two of my favorite eating places are Captain Anderson's, owned by Jimmy and Johnny Patronis, and The Sunset, owned by Charles Collins. We are always treated to marvelous meals at these restaurants.

My husband and children usually went along on our beach trips while we taped our segments for the show. It was during one of our elaborate dinners at Captain Anderson's, that I realized both of my sons had ordered the most expensive item on the menu - steak and lobster! I leaned down to correct them on their choice when Trant responded, "Gee, Mom, this is free! It doesn't cost us anything!" Thankfully, our host, Johnny Patronis, who overheard this remark, thought it was funny. He readily assured the boys that they could order whatever they wanted. (I think they both got two desserts each.)

Johnny Patronis is a very forgiving man because soon after that, I was doing a feature on Captain Anderson's Restaurant having received the coveted "Golden Spoon" award for excellence in dining. As I held the spoon up, (while balancing my microphone with the other hand), I dropped and broke the "Golden Spoon" right in the middle of the interview.

"Oh, no!" I moaned. "I've broken the Golden Spoon". Johnny just rolled with laughter, and so did my cameraman. Thank goodness, all I broke was the little wire hinges that held the spoon on the plaque. Later, in honor of Johnny Patronis's birthday, I played the "blooper" for our audience. Actually, I think the Patronis brothers liked it more than the interview I had aired originally.

Another great story that happened at Captain Anderson's was one that occured when Tony and I both were doing the interview. We were in the kitchen "helping" with the desserts. Tony was being silly getting frosting all over him while I was trying to keep a straight face. For some reason, I was under the impression that the head cake maker, who prepared those wonderful pecan meal cakes was unable to speak English. I kept making hand gestures for him to show us how he prepared his recipe. The more he looked puzzled, the more I believed he couldn't understand what I was saying. At last, in frustration, the chef spoke up, "Mrs. Varnum, if you'll just tell me what you want, I'll try to do it!"

Well, that did it. I was already tickled at Tony, and when I discovered how stupid I had been to think the chef couldn't speak English, I started laughing so hard I couldn't get control of myself for some time. Laughter is contagious, as you well know, because by then, the entire kitchen staff was laughing hysterically. (I can't believe they still let me eat there!)

...

The CBS Star interviews were always scheduled in the early summer, so one year, we invited Kay Bruner from the new *Dothan Progress*, a bi-weekly newspaper, to go with me in order to do write ups on the stars. This was the beginning of a friendship that continues until today.

At a later date, I introduced Kay to my friend James Robison, who was in Dothan for a one night evangelistic rally. James was so impressed with Kay's writing skills, that he hired her to write for his *Life's Answer* magazine. This proved to be just what God ordered for Kay because she finally found the <u>answer</u> for her own life - a personal relationship with Jesus Christ. Kay is now happily married to pharmacist Rey Moreno, and when she is not taking care of business for their pharmacies or looking after their four children, she edits for Christian publishing firms.

...

"The Silver Eagles" was one of the army's most prestigious helicopter teams. One morning we featured them on our program, and afterwards, I was invited to fly with them over Dothan. I had chosen to wear a long silk skirt that morning, not knowing I would be boarding a helicopter. I must have been a great sight to see, attempting to climb up into the helicopter while also trying to keep my skirt down. At last, I managed to get in. Next, the pilot put the big helmet on my hair which mashed my hair down. We could only communicate through the speaker and the head sets on our helmets. It was really exciting! He also let me "blow smoke" over Dothan.

Right in the middle of our flight, I did a dumb thing. I noticed he wasn't wearing a wedding band, so I asked him if he were married. He looked so shocked, because, I guess he thought I was making a pass at him.

Reading his thoughts, I quickly pointed to my own wedding band, and explained, "Oh, no, it's not for me. I'm happily married. I was just thinking about my friend Betty Ramsey." He assured me he was also happily married. (Why do I always do these stupid things?)

...

Art Creamer had worked at WTVY since it first went on the air in 1955. He and his family owned Creamer's, a very fashionable ladies clothing store. Art asked me to do a commercial for him around Easter. It consisted of wearing one of his dresses and ad-libbing a spot. It must have worked because someone bought the dress literally "right off my back."

After I did many of Creamer's spots, Hilma Green called me to do some commercials for Hilma's. I loved trying on beautiful clothes, choosing selections to show on TV and visiting with Miss Hilma. She often tried to put me in smaller dresses than I could wear when she wanted a particular style shown. We soon became very good friends and often prayed together about situations she was having to face.

In addition to Hilma's, I started doing commercials for Joyce Clark at Nicole's , Grace Kirkland at Grace's Fads N Fashions, Liz Lambert at Kennington's, David Ethridge at D'Ethridge, and for a short time, The Cottage. There was a time when I did a "live" spot each day with a different outfit to wear.

Whenever anyone has to do a live spot, you never know what might happen. Sometimes, I've had dresses to slip off the hangers right in the middle of a commercial. When it's live you just go right on. I am so thankful, though, that I never said the wrong store name, no matter how many different ones I was advertising for. Since I ad-libbed all my spots, I did make up some rather unusual names for colors. Hilma always waited to see what I might call one of her newest fashion shades. I never knew myself until it popped out either.

Kim's was also one of my clients and even though it was an infant and toddler shop, I thoroughly enjoyed doing their spots. Once I had a polka dot dress to show, and I mentioned that I had also worn one like that as a child. .That dress sold immediately.

Eventually, Sam Jones at Sam Jones Mobile Homes got me to do some spots for him. Many I ad-libbed. I sang in one. (My children begged me never to do this again.) One day I added, "Please go see Sam!" It became his slogan. Everywhere Sam went, he got teased about "Please go see Sam!"

...

General William J. Maddox was one of the most popular and most colorful generals at Ft. Rucker. It was such a thrill to interview him! The first time I met him, he requested some water. Hazel, our station maid, went all out with a pitcher of ice water and paper cups. Instead of picking up the cup and pouring from the pitcher, I tried pouring the water directly into the cup sitting on the table which turned the cup completely over. I was so embarrassed, but it amused the General.

We called General Maddox, "The Silver Fox". He often piloted his helicopter directly to WTVY whenever he was scheduled for an interview. One morning I walked into the snack bar, and General Maddox was making coffee. It was obvious his staff greatly admired him as much as we did.

General Maddox's wife was a truly beautiful, gracious lady. Jaye Maddox was the product of an American mother and a Japanese father. The famous author, James Michener, had visited in their home in Japan many times. In fact, earlier, he had told Rex and me all about how Jaye's Japanese father had been so angered when Japan attacked Pearl Harbor. Jaye's father had intended to promote peace between the two countries and had even been in Washington at the time of the attack in negotiations with our President, Franklin Roosevelt.

After the war, Jaye had met the handsome army officer, Bill Maddox, had fallen in love and married him. Jaye had followed her husband through all his promotions and tours of duty. Now, they were at Ft. Rucker for their latest assignment.

Many times the lovely Mrs. Maddox called me to ask my advice on everything from where to shop to what TV set I would recommend. I was often invited to eat in their home also. My favorite part of the meal was when she would ring a bell and a "house boy" (military aid) would come immediately to fulfill her requests. (I told my husband that I wanted a "house boy" for Christmas.)

For years after the Maddoxes left Ft. Rucker, we still corresponded. General Maddox had opted to retire from the service when his superior officers assigned him to a post in the Pentagon. A desk job was just not right for Bill Maddox. Instead, he went to work as an instructor for military operations in some Middle Eastern countries.

...

The Officers Wives Club at Ft. Rucker invited me to come to their annual fashion show. Cindy O'Brien was assigned to do the story for our news department, on that account, we rode up together. Cindy was having a grand time chatting with all the ladies while we were all eating together. When the fashion show started, I noticed that Cindy had made no effort to get her camera.

At last I could stand it no longer. "Cindy, aren't you going to tape some of the show?" I quizzed her. I noticed she looked at me strangely. Reluctantly, she got up and began putting her camera and tri-pod together. I decided to try to help her.

"Cindy," I questioned when she began taping the show. "You forgot your lights."

"I forgot the tape, too." She muttered out of the side of her mouth.

"You what?" I replied. "Then, why on earth are you pretending to tape this?" I asked.

"Just faking it," she grinned. "They were expecting a TV camera, so here it is." (I wonder if they tried to catch the coverage on WTVY?)

...

Tony Scott and I always enjoyed covering the annual National Peanut Festival. We had all the queens, celebrities and competitors on "The Morning Show" during the celebration.

My first encounter with country comedian Jerry Clower was at a Wednesday night festival event. One minute he was serious and the next, he was clowning. After my interview, Jerome and I stayed for Jerry's show. It was so funny! The peanut festival crowd packed out the place to listen to Jerry's stories of all his exploits. I only wish Tony could have been with us. Jerry Clower and Tony Scott together would be just too, too much.

On Saturday, we always covered the National Peanut Festival Parade. People would often try to talk to us while we were on the air. Every year Nick Saad brought us peanuts and something to drink during the parade. What a special gesture!

Many times during the parade, floats would get out of order, and no matter how hard the ham radio team tried, the names still got confused. We honestly did the best that we could to announce the correct float or vehicle as it appeared on TV, but on Monday mornings, we got telephone calls complaining about something. I guess we must enjoy criticism, because we still cover the parade every year.

Memorable characters that always appeared in the parade include: Toby, the clown who was sad faced and never talked, skating Dave, Tri-State area bands, the new National Peanut Festival Queen and court, Lindsey Hall's dancers, Couch's peanut trucks, the Mobile Trail Maidens (all decked out in antebellum gowns), the area media, politicians running for office, the reigning queens from all the wiregrass towns, the Corvette Club, Mascots for commercial businesses such as the Piggly Wiggly Pig and Ronald McDonald, and always at the end, the horses! (Well, after that the clean up crew came along.)

...

Two of my favorite singing groups appeared at the Dothan Civic Center, The Imperials and the Statler Brothers. When the Imperials were performing, Russ Taff, one of the lead singers gave me the scoop on his leaving the group. I don't think the other singers knew about this until he announced it during our interview. At least, they all gave the impression that they were surprised at his statement.

The Statler Brothers were riding a wave of popularity when they came through Dothan. Their harmony is equal to none, and their combination of wonderful music and humor make a great show. Harold and Don, the brothers, provided a zany interview. Lou and Phil were also very informative. I think I was one of the last to interview the group before Lou had to leave the Statler Brothers due to his serious health problems.

...

Auburn football greats Terry Beasley and John "Rat " Riley visited our "Morning Show" also. These were special interviews for me as I'm an Auburn fan. John had been a close personal friend of mine, and he took the time that morning to play some football with my son Trant out back. Once, I even had the opportunity to interview Legendary Auburn Football Coach "Shug" Jordan. He was a prince of a gentleman. His memory will be cherished by both Auburn and Alabama fans alike, just like Coach "Bear" Bryant's will be.

...

Mr. Woods had started encouraging me to do documentaries which could air on our regular time slot or even at another time. One of the first specials we taped was at a Methodist Group Home for girls in Pensacola, Florida. Bobby "Red" Flournoy went with me to do the taping.

These girls appeared, on the surface, like any other normal teenager. We were so saddened to learn of some of their histories. Some had been abused sexually and physically, and others had a background of alcohol and drug abuse. A few of the girls had scrapes with the law.

Our taping had to be done with the girls shot in the distance or with their backs to the camera. They were allowed to talk to us off camera. The program was a success because it depicted an actual story about changing the lives of young people. My reward was getting to know all the girls. Even "Red" was visibly touched. It had taken us an entire week-end with them to do the special like I wanted.

When it aired, we really got a lot of favorable response. After presenting a copy to the executive director of the Methodist Group Homes, Roy McLouglin, we felt that our mission had been completed.

Was I ever surprised when I was given a special commendation from the United Methodist Church and Dr. Floyd Enfinger, the District Superintendent. They even surprised me "on the air" to make the presentation.

That year I also got to interview author Josh McDowell who was brought to Dothan by the Dothan Association of Evangelical Christians. I had read his books, *More Than a Carpenter* and *Evidence That Demands a Verdict* . Mr. McDowell made quite an impact on all who attended his meeting that night. Mr. McDowell had been a super intellectual, who, on a dare by Christian students, set out to prove that Jesus Christ was a hoax. Instead, he came to believe that Jesus was exactly who He said He was. Because of his search and discovery, Josh McDowell has now impacted thousands of lives as he travels literally all over the world to speak about his faith.

One of his most interesting stories took place "behind the Iron Curtain." Josh had received an invitation to speak to a communist group. When he arrived, he was placed at the front of the room with many spotlights shining on him. The rest of the room was pitch black. Voices from all over the room asked him pointed questions about this "religion" that he professed. In his heart, Josh believed that these people, who chose to remain in the dark, were actual "seekers" who wanted very much to hear about his God. Because of the communist hierarchy, perhaps they were also afraid of being punished for this interest. Josh said he literally felt the Holy Spirit directing his every word. Whatever happened after he left, only God knows. All at once, Josh told me, he was ushered out as quickly as he had been rushed in. Other stories he shared during his message were just as dynamic. I even re-ran the interview with Josh McDowell more than once because it was so filled with such incredible events.

...

Late one night Jerome and I got a telephone call from one of our regular "Morning Show" guests, Dr. William C. Adams, Director of the Medical Center's Emergency department. Dr. Adams told us that Jerry Vann, my dear friend, had suffered a massive heart attack. Jerry was stable, Dr. Adams explained, but still in critical condition. We thanked Dr. Adams for calling us and Jerome and I started to pray. I think we prayed the rest of the night.

The next morning, I was so torn between going to work and rushing to the hospital to see about Jerry. I knew, realistically, that I had to do the show because Tony was not prepared. In retrospect, I honestly don't know how I made it through the program, ("Sunny Side Up", I guess).

As soon as the show ended, I was out the back door and on my way to the hospital.

I had the strongest urge that I simply had to get to Jerry and pray for him. I was fully aware that there was nothing special about me or my prayers, but I knew I had to see him.

I stopped at the front desk and was told that Jerry Vann was in the Cardiac Intensive Care Unit. I hurriedly ran to the elevator and exited on the second floor. I ran into a friend who told me that I was in the wrong place. She then gave me some additional instructions as I rushed over to the nearest elevator.

Believe this or not, but just then, the elevator door opened and two men were trying to get a patient on a stretcher out of the elevator. One look and I knew. It was Jerry Vann. Jerry was asleep, and for some reason, the two men had the stretcher stuck half in the elevator and half out. I put my hand on Jerry's arm and prayed as hard as I could under my breath. Just as I finished, the men were able to get the stretcher out, and they rushed him off through two doors. The greatest sense of peace filled my heart. I knew Jerry would live.

Because he later had to have open heart surgery, the Vanns decided to have it done in Dothan. "They surely wouldn't let anything happen to WTVY's New Director," Jerry told his wife Barbara. Later, I stayed with Barbara all during his surgery, even though I was sick with the flu. I shared with Barbara the scripture that God had given me concerning Jerry. It was Psalms 91:15: "He will call upon me, and I will answer him; I will be with him in trouble. I will deliver him and honor him. With long life will I satisfy him and show him my salvation."

Jerry did survive the surgery, even though we went through some trying moments. At the present time, Jerry is still one of WTVY's most valuable assets. He works harder than anyone!

...

Tony Barber was a Baptist preacher's son and WTVY's art director. He was also given the job of being one of our "Morning Show" cameramen when Johnny Williford left. Tony was always in my prayers because he was now assigned to go with me to do specials. If I had ever seen someone literally "running from the Lord", it was Tony Barber.

Many of the interviews I did on location were with dedicated Christians, like Larry Burkett, who taught people how to manage money the Biblical way. Once, a visiting missionary insisted on Tony joining us in prayer after the interview. For some reason, the man must have sensed what God had planned for Tony Barber's life because the entire prayer was all for Tony.

It was not long after this, that Tony surrendered his life to God. I'll always remember the time he shared this with me. We both cried for joy. He was not with WTVY very long after his conversion, because Tony Barber knew that God had called him to preach. Tony is now a Baptist pastor just like his father.

...

Not only did Jerry Vann survive his medical problems, but one Sunday morning, he gave his heart to God at a small Baptist church in Cowarts, Alabama, shortly after Tony Barber got saved. It was Tony who met me the next day at work to tell me about what had happened to Jerry.

"Don't let him know I told you," Tony said. "I know he'll want to tell you himself."

Jerry did come and tell me. Again, I cried.

Chapter Seven
On the road

After Fob James's first term in office he chose not to run for re-election. This allowed Chris Bence to come back to work at WTVY-FM full time. Tony Scott was now able to do more with me on "The Morning Show", as he was relieved of his radio duties. Teresa Thomas also joined us to do the community announcements.

It was evident that we had to expand our coverage in order to keep good quality programs; therefore, in addition to doing programs at Panama City Beach, we moved to Destin and Ft. Walton as well.

Wayne Register, WTVY production director at the time, would usually go with me on these trips. Once, in Destin, I had to do a feature walking down the beach fully clothed while my guests were wearing bathing suits. Ever since I had been diagnosed with lupus, I was not allowed to get much exposure to the sun. I'm sure I looked funny with my long sleeves and long pants on. (I would have looked even funnier in a bathing suit.)

One February in Ft. Walton it was so cold that I had to wear a big furry coat while we taped a feature on a fishing boat going down the river. Wayne was afraid if we tipped over I would drown in that big coat. Obviously, that was not a good time to do a beach show.

Barbara Hall was WTVY's sales representative for Ft. Walton for awhile and scheduled us for still another special on this beautiful city. This time "Red" Flournoy and his wife Phyllis traveled with me. Barbara had us scheduled to eat at a very famous restaurant right on the beach. "Red" kept encouraging his wife to "order whatever she wanted" because it was on the house.

As it turned out, Barbara had not properly communicated with the restaurant owner, and we were given the huge check. None of us had any money with us, so we were all in a quandary as to what to do without being embarrassed. "Red" suggested we "wash dishes" or "hock our coats" that they had already checked for us when we first came in. Dothan Theater owner Rufus Davis and some of his friends came in just then. We even considered asking him for a loan. By this time, we were all laughing so hard, that, I'm sure the people in the restaurant thought we were drunk. (Really none of us had anything alcoholic to drink.)

By and by, Barbara remembered that she had a credit card and they took that. WTVY re-imbursed her later. Never again has that happened because I always make sure that the restaurant owner is aware that since we tape a feature on their restaurant at no charge, they, in turn, provide us with a meal. Most people are delighted at this arrangement.

...

Claire Valetto, one of my high school friends, invited us to do a special on Pensacola. It didn't seem to matter that it was technically out of range as the feature was well received. There is so much history involved in the development of this city that we decided to compare the beginning of Pensacola to what it has become in our present day.

...

When the Ashford High School Band planned to go to Washington, D. C. , Wayne Register and I asked our boss if we could go along and do some features in Washington. Mr. Woods agreed. After confirmation of our trip we contacted one of my old high school buddies, Johnny Jenkins, who was now in the Pentagon to ask for his help in setting up interviews.

Security at the Pentagon is always tight, so whenever we entered, we had to properly identify ourselves. Wayne and I had media passes, but when my husband went through the entrance, he told them that he was only there to check out the "Tab machines and the bathrooms for his wife". The look on that guard's face said it all! I grabbed Jerome's arm and told the man that he was with us.

These "mini-documentaries", as we dubbed them, turned out just like we had hoped. Johnny got us right into the Pentagon to interview General Pustay, the man who had been in charge of the aborted effort to rescue our captured American citizens from Iran. It was a difficult interview, but I had been prepared for it by Colonel Richard Able, special assistant to the Chairman of the Joint Chiefs of Staff, General Jones.

Colonel Able was a dedicated Christian who had helped form the Fellowship of Christian Athletes organization at the Air Force Academy when he was there. He not only provided me with a good interview himself, but he made sure I got to talk to everyone I needed to meet.

John Jenkins is a very tall, stately man, who had worked in Army Intelligence for years. His fellow officers really gave him a hard time when I referred to him in my Southern voice as "John ee". At one point during our visit, Wayne's camera developed some problems. John then arranged for the Army's TV trainees to tape our segments at the Pentagon. Since the military was not allowed to lend us equipment, John came up with the idea of using this opportunity as a "training lesson" for the new TV crew at the Pentagon.

Standing on the capital steps, I interviewed many of the Senators and Congressmen about issues that related particularly to Alabama. Early one morning, Wayne noticed that I did my whole interview with a certain guest with my eyes closed. Afterwards, he suggested we change locations so the sun wouldn't get in my eyes.

"Wayne", I confided, as I wiped off my face, "It wasn't the sun, that gentleman was spitting on me while he talked. I shut my eyes so it wouldn't get in my eyes". Did we ever have a good laugh over that experience!

John Jenkins and his wife Ernestine were marvelous hosts and showed us all the Washington landmarks. Wayne and I made sure that we covered the Ashford High School band's performance on the capitol steps since Wayne and Donna Register's daughters, Robin and Kaye, were members of the band.

...

At one point in time, WTVY management decided to move our "Morning Show" back to 6:00 a.m. and make it a part of "Good Morning Tri- States with Gene Ragan and Red Holland. That's when Wayne Register and I started our all-out effort to tape as much as possible. We visited area restaurants, Grandpa's Attic (a local consignment store), Iron City, Georgia; Westville in Lumpkin, Georgia; and we even did a special on a young television repairman who wanted to be a country singer. Wherever we went, we were welcomed by all the local townspeople.

Then one day, Red Holland invited me to go fishing with him. I told him I would do it but challenged him to go to my beauty parlor for a new hairdo and skin care treatment first. He went and loved every minute of it! The girls at the Kutt Above enjoyed pampering Red. They even talked him into cutting off his sideburns!

Next, it was my turn. I am certainly no fisherman. Red, Wayne Register and I set up the camera on Red's boat in the middle of a private pond. Red soon discovered that he had to "bait" my hook. The poor crickets kept "looking" at me, and I couldn't bring myself to stab those worms. When I did catch the first fish, I stood up in order to pull it in and Red said that I almost turned us over. He was really having fun with me.

Being the jokester that he is, Red even had a game warden planted out in the trees taking pictures of us. When Red told me I was fishing without a license, I threw the pole back to him and declared that, "I was doing a television show!"

Red really laughed at this. He had played this prank to illustrate why everyone - no matter what - must have a fishing license. Of course, he had already purchased one for me that morning so I would be "legal" when we fished. I'm not sure anyone would believe that the description on the license was actually mine. It read: Ann Varnum, 5' 2" tall, weight: 105, Blonde hair and blue eyes! (Thanks Red for the flattery! I even forgave him for his joke on me regarding the "lurking' game warden.)

No matter how many times we have aired our fishing show, people still request it again. It was truly a funny show.

At another time, we taped a cooking segment with Red at his home in Webb. Red is an excellent biscuit maker and showed us how simple it really is to make biscuits. We were flooded with requests for Red's biscuit recipe after that. One viewer wrote that she believed Red's recipe had "saved her marriage" now that she could make biscuits.

Presently, my husband and I have the good fortune of living in Red's old home. His prized fish collection still hangs on the walls in our den. When Red moved to Panama City, he didn't have room for a lot of things. (Who would have ever believed this strange turn of events?) My sister Martha and her husband Jack are our business partners and co-own, with us, "The Field O' Dreams Farm". They plan to build here on the other side of the pond when Jack retires from Kimberly Clark.

...

One of our Ft. Walton sales representatives sold a package to a group from the Greek Orthodox Church. To fulfill their contract, Wayne Register and I had to go to St. Augustine, Florida to tape an hour special on some of their shrines. We had to really co-ordinate our planning with the church to make sure everything we did was acceptable to them.

St. Augustine is a beautiful, historic city filled with mystery. To fully capture our story, we took the cameras down the old cobblestone streets, as I narrated our story on various locations. The Ave' Maria Grotto was breathtaking with it's dazzling artifacts and paintings.

"Corky" our sales representative, told us one morning that we were to cover a wedding ceremony inside the historic grotto. We were instructed as to what we could do and what we could not do. The Greek Orthodox Church wanted the complete ceremony on tape. Therefore, we had to get in position and wait.

As the marriage began, Wayne started the cameras. Closer and closer he moved while he attempted to catch the words of the priest, as well as the expressions on the faces of the couple. What none of us could have expected was what happened next. The priest began to chant. Then, he started "shaking out" holy oil or holy water all over the gathered group. It was the camera that got it full force. Wayne couldn't move in either direction because others in the wedding party had closed ranks behind him.

When we got back to our motel, we examined the camera. It survived, but when we looked at the tape, it was obvious when the holy oil had splattered on the camera lens. (Some clever editing back at the station was able to take care of this problem in spite of the blurred images.)

During that trip, I developed "inner ear" problems and felt dizzy most of the time. Somehow, with Wayne's encouragement, I made it through the feature. We covered pearl divers, Old Spanish forts, vintage landmarks, and, of course, the religious ceremonies of the Greek Orthodox Church. When we presented the Church a copy of our hour special, they seemed to be pleased. It certainly did make a very good historical documentary.

...

The next big trip Wayne and I made was to Jamaica. A Jamaican plantation owner, Jack Wilmont, had paid all our expenses so that we could do a TV feature on his operation. We also planned to do a documentary on a Jamaican orphanage run by an American preacher and his wife while we were there.

The flight over was very pleasant, but everything changed the minute we touched down in Montego Bay, Jamaica. Going through customs was a disaster. It seems that the preacher had failed to get a permit to allow our TV equipment to be admitted into the country. It was also obvious that the inspectors wanted a bribe. I was determined not to pay them anything, no matter what. So, we did what we always do in an emergency, we prayed.

In a few minutes, I walked back over to the counter. A second man had joined the first man who had been giving us such a hard time.

In my most pleasant voice, I smiled, and said, "Look, we had no idea our hosts had not made arrangements for our TV equipment to be admitted. (One customs agent had told us they couldn't let us take our camera in because of the black market. He said that we might be trying to "sell" this equipment inside their country illegally.) We are here to do two television specials. Jack Wilmont has paid our expenses to come here and after all, you can keep us in Jamaica if we don't have our television equipment when we start for home!"

The two men looked at each other and the new man said, "Okay, Lady," and stamped our papers. I was elated! God must have given me just the right words, or the name "Jack Wilmont" might have changed their minds. Whatever the case, we were on our way.

Right outside the terminal, we met our next challenge. The preacher had rented a very small, two door Volkswagen to carry us to our destination. It took an hour to tie our equipment, suit cases and other stuff on top of the car. All four of us squeezed into the car with the preacher and held our breath.

He took off in a spin talking and laughing as he went. We kept looking at each other as he sped through town and headed for the mountains. "Slow down", I finally urged. "You're going to have a wreck!"

"Oh, no," he assured us. "There is no speed limit in Jamaica. Everyone drives like this!"

"I don't care!" I instructed, "if we lose that equipment, our boss will never forgive us!"

He slowed down just a little but as he headed up into the hills, he sped up again.

"Where are we going?" I finally asked.

"Just wait and see," he smiled. "Have we got a surprise for you!"

Did he ever have a surprise for us! When at last, we arrived at our accommodations, we were in a state of shock. In front of us was a simple block house. The front door opened and out came ten of the most adorable little Jamaican children we had ever seen. They were all clapping, singing and waving their greetings to us. Our hearts melted.

Yes, we were to spend our time in Jamaica at the orphanage. There was no air conditioning, no hot water and even though Jerome and I slept on a three quarter bed, Wayne and Donna Register slept on a bunk bed together. It was quite an experience.

We had to take showers often because the climate was so hot and humid, but the water that was piped down from a mountain stream was ice cold. The soap never lathered either. When any of us showered, we squealed all through our baths.

Getting to know the children was worth everything we went through. To tell the truth, if we could have, we would have loaded them all up and brought them home with us.

Our suitcases were filled with gifts for the orphans. Donna and I had also brought our Tabs. Honestly, we lived on Tabs and the peanut butter we had brought for the children while we were there. Needless to say, the Jamaican food was quite different from ours.

The next morning after our arrival, we got up prepared for work. Jamaican dignitaries began pouring in to the orphanage. Princess Lawes was in charge of the children's services. In Jamaica, there is no welfare system. Provisions were made in their country only for orphans and the elderly who had no family.

It seemed that I was doing interviews with the entire Jamaican population. Soon, it began to dawn on us. This preacher was "using us" to gain favor with all the authorities in government who had to "oversee" his orphanage. No matter the difficulty, we had no choice; we went right along with his plan. It was a long, hard day so sleep came easy that night.

The next morning we headed out for Jack Wilmont's plantation. On the way, we had to go through "Fern Gully." True, it was a beautiful passageway through lush, green foliage. The problem was the continuous circular drive round and round and round. We were all stuffed into that tiny Volkswagen with our equipment strapped to the top. There was no air conditioning, and as we went round and round, we all began to get very sick.

We had to stop to try to get back our stability. It was too late for Wayne Register. He was throwing up continuously, and he was also very dizzy. What could we do? We had to do the television documentary with the man who paid for our trip. Again, we prayed.

Soon, Wayne was able to get back into the car. We had to drive very slowly but in a short time we arrived at the plantation. Wayne had to lie down while the rest of us were treated to the best meal we had eaten all week.

The Wilmont plantation consisted of a thriving restaurant, a Jamaican Zoo and a farm that was unbelievable. The family home was perched on the side of a mountain with a huge Olympic-sized pool overlooking the farming operations. After our meal, we were carried on a guided tour through the entire plantation.

Wayne was still trying to get well enough to do his camera work. It seemed impossible. Jerome was a good still photographer, but he knew nothing about a video camera. We continued to pray. Finally, Wayne was able to get up and set the camera up with Jerome's assistance. With God's help, we were able to do the taping. Jack Wilmont was a kindly host who reminded us of a larger version of Harry Bellafonte. His wife was an elegant Jamaiican lady who carried herself like a princess. Visiting the Wilmont Complex was an adventure we'll never forget. (Fern Gully was an experience Wayne Register will never forget either.) It was a long trip back to the orphanage to say the least.

When we had finished all of our taping, it was time to go home. We insisted that the preacher carry us to Montego Bay so that we could spend the night at the big hotel before we had to fly out. I guess we were getting a little "battle" worn at this point. When we arrived at our destination, there was only one room available. We took it!

We were so thankful that there were two double beds in the room. We didn't sleep much that night because we were all laughing and sharing about the many crazy things that had happened to us during the trip.

The next morning we had to go through customs again. Could we get our television equipment home? That was the big question. We prayed. An entirely different man was at the counter. He seemed to hesitate momentarily, and then, he stamped our papers. We almost ran to the plane.

When we got back home, we realized that America had never looked better to us. The first place we stopped after we landed was at a Quincey's restaurant. Food had never tasted so good either. The four of us agreed that from then on, the furtherest place south of Dothan for awhile would be Panama City, Florida.

...

Charles Woods had returned to Dothan from his latest venture in the San Diego Real Estate Market only to discover that he had to have surgery again. Jerome and I were staying with him in the hospital before he was to be taken to the surgical suite. As the anesthesia was beginning to work, Mr. Woods muttered something about sending me and Wayne Register to California to talk to a woman who fed the hungry. Because he was medicated at the time, I didn't think he knew what he was saying.

Was I ever surprised when the first statement that he made after he was regaining consciousness, was a continuation of what he had said earlier. He announced that Wayne and I were to make plans to fly to Los Angeles very soon to meet Mom Taylor, a very unusual lady (as we were to learn later).

During our flight to L. A., I remember turning to Wayne and stating, "Wayne, I do hope we get to stay in a nice motel on this trip."

He laughed, "Me too!"

Mom Taylor met us at the airport. She was a big talker, but we immediately liked her. Contrary to the preacher we had met in Jamaica, she was a genuinely good person. (I didn't mention the preacher's name because his church later brought him up on charges for using funds personally that had been given for the orphanage.)

Mom took us to two very nice motel rooms. I slept like a baby.

Taping the Mom Taylor story took us three days. Mr. Woods wanted it aired on all the TV stations that he now owned. There was just so much to do. How could we best explain what this woman did? We started with people who told of their involvement with this wonderful lady. Next, we taped the food storage places, the food pick up sites, and, we worked until we had everything we needed. It was going to be a very difficult show to edit, though.

Mom Taylor was not a wealthy woman, but she had a heart for poor people. "Those who give to the poor lend to the Lord," she would quote from the Bible. Somehow, she had managed to motivate people, including large chain grocery stores, to give her food. Sometimes, she even received donations of clothing and household goods. With all of these gifts, she found a needy person to give them to.

Before we left, Mom had started loading me and Wayne down with trinkets. The more we tried to keep her from giving us things, the more she insisted. She was one of the most loving and giving persons I'd ever met.

We found ourselves a little reluctant to leave this great lady, but we had another assignment. We were to meet Joe Earl Holloway in Texas to tape the Troy State University football game that was to be played that Saturday night in a way out of the way stadium in Lousianna.

As we were boarding the plane that morning to leave Los Angeles, Wayne and I noticed men walking around with signs which read: "All the pilots who work for this airline are on strike, who is flying your plane?"

"Wayne," I whispered, "That is so ridiculous! You know the airlines would have to have a good pilot to fly this plane, or they would get sued!"

After take-off, Wayne and I considered being the first to sue. It was a very rocky ride, and then when we were coming in for a landing in Texas, whoever was flying the plane dropped so quickly that it caused us to feel excruciating pain in both our ears! (The moral of this story is never fly until you know who your pilot is.)

We met Joe Earl along the side of the road literally. Joe had ridden to Texas with the Troy State University team. They had to go on, so they told him where to stay until we arrived. I was so glad we were not late.

It was a long ride to the college campus in Thibodaux, Louisiana, where we were to do the Troy State game. When we arrived, it was a very windy night. I was getting really cold and my hair was blowing wildly in the wind. To top it all off, Troy lost the game.

Wayne, Joe and I left right after the wrap-up of the ball game and drove straight through to Dothan. We had to have the tape back to air on the Troy State Football program that Sunday. It was a long, hard night. I tried to sleep in the back seat of the station wagon on the way home. Wayne and Joe said I "snored". (I probably did.) We arrived in Dothan just as the sun came up. Again, there's no place like home.

...

Joe Earl had to do the camera work on our next assignment. It was to Lakeland, Florida this time. Mr. Woods' daughter, Ruth Ellen, had met a couple who did foster care for severely handicapped children. Some of these children, they had even adopted. Ruthie was so impressed with the work that Pat and Gerald Foster did that she convinced her father that their story needed to be told.

What Joe and I found was beyond our expectations. There were eight children in the home with special needs. Two had spina bifada, three were profoundly retarded, two had cerebral palsy and one, whom they had adopted, was fully grown (17 or 18 years of age) and was still in diapers in a huge crib. It was a very difficult situation to handle professionally because of our compassion for these special children.

Joe and I were both very touched by the quality of care the children received, and, more than that, the genuine love we felt that was expressed between the couple and the children.

Each of the children, according to their abilities, had certain jobs to perform. All tasks were done cheerfully, and seemingly, with great pride. Many times, one child had to assist another one in combing his hair and brushing his teeth. Each time we would put the camera on the children, they would giggle with excitement.

We had arrived early that morning in order to see how they all managed to get ready for school. Six of the eight children were able to attend a nearby school, and it was obvious that their morning duties were done routinely and not just to impress us. When the last chore was done, all six of the children were out front in time for the bus which arrived about 7:15 a.m. (It was equipped with lifts for the students in wheelchairs.)

As soon as we got the youngsters off to school, Pat and Gerald told us each child's story. Some of the children had been abandoned by their parents when it was discovered that they had serious birth defects. The teenage boy who was still in the over-sized crib was one who had been abandoned. That's why the couple had adopted him.

No matter how complex his handicap, Jamie was greatly loved by the entire family. They talked to him as if he understood every word they said, and, perhaps, he did. I know that the entire experience will always be a reminder to me of the power of unconditional love.

...

Never did I realize that doing some of these specials would be a preliminary to facing something very traumatic in my own family. No one ever thinks that tragedy could strike them or their loved ones in an instant. I certainly never thought about this possibility. When it did happen to us, all we could do was pray.

Jerome and I received a call late one night that our nephew had been severely injured in a diving accident. Jack had only been at Auburn University four days when he decided to take a late night swim in the pool at the trailer park where he lived. He dived in and hit his head on the bottom of the pool.

When my sister Martha called, the medical team was preparing to transfer him to Atlanta. Jerome and I got up, dressed and left to be with our family. We prayed all the way to the hospital.

Jack had injured two of his vertebrae-level C5 and C6. He was left a quadriplegic. We kept praying for a miracle until grim reality finally set in. Our next effort was to get Jack the best care possible. Through some rather unusual circumstances, we were able to get Jack admitted to the Shepherd Spinal Center.

After seeing what was being done at this great hospital to help my nephew Jack, I knew I wanted to do a special on this wonderful facility. Mr. Woods said we could do it, so Phillip Bump and I drove to Atlanta to tape the story. It was difficult, on my part, to stay focused on my work because my emotions were so close to the surface as we taped Jack trying to accomplish the simple tasks that he was being taught to do. This was my flesh and blood, and I loved him very much. Many times I had to fight back the tears in order to continue.

When the Shepherd Spinal Center Documentary was completed, Mr. Woods not only allowed me to air it at WTVY, but he sent it to all of his other stations also. It ran in Evansville, Indiana; West Monroe, Louisiana; Lubbock, Texas and Springfield, Missouri. When all the phone calls began pouring in to the Shepherd Spinal Center, the medical team could not believe the response. Phil and I were particularly pleased with the way it had turned out.

After Jack completed all the programs available to him at Shepherd's, he returned to his parents' home in Alpharetta, Georgia. His life seemed to come to a dead end until one day he heard about Walker Institute in Los Angeles, California. In spite of the a complex venture,

Jack's parents made arrangements for him to go check it out.

I took a vacation and went with my sister Martha to carry Jack to Los Angeles. After we talked with the directors at Walker, we knew that Jack could receive additional help there.

Some time later, after Jack had been going through the various programs at the clinic for a few months, he saw a television crew taping a special on Walker Institute. He confided in some of the physical therapists that his Aunt Ann worked at a television station and had taped a special at Shepherd Spinal Center.

The remark got back to the founder of Walker Institute herself. After the first TV documentary did not turn out like Dr. Walker had expected, I received an invitation to come back to California to tape a warmer, less sterile presentation.

In a short time after this request, I was on my way back to Los Angeles to tape still another special with my nephew Jack. On this trip, I had none of my television cameramen with me. Dr. Walker had hired the same video company who had originally produced the informational tape on the Institute to work with me. To be honest, I was very nervous about working with a totally different crew.

Doing a show with this California production team was very difficult! My camera operators had always worked with me - almost anticipating where I was headed next. They would have never stopped me right in the middle of a sentence to move a camera for a "different angle" or for different lighting.

By the time I was into my third interview, every guest was a nervous wreck, and so was I. When it came time for me to tape the segment with my nephew Jack in the orthopedic braces that would give him the sense of walking again, I could no longer take the pressure.

I burst out with, "Look, I know you are a professional team, but I am interested in getting the real story here. Don't stop me, or that camera again even if I fall flat on my face on the floor!"

Because of my insistence, the cameras continued to roll, as I went into my remarks concerning what Jack was experiencing there at Walker. As he began to "move" up the bar with help from his therapist, I spoke what was on my heart. My voice broke, genuine tears spilled down my face but I continued until I knew I had said all I needed to say. I called for the cameras to stop. No one in the room said a word.

When I got back to Dothan, Phillip Bump and I worked for hours editing the raw footage that had been taped by the California production crew. The only part we didn't edit was the final scene with Jack on the "standing braces", and my personal comments. We added the theme song from *The Man of La Mancha* "To Dream The Impossible Dream" in the background as Jack struggled up the ramp. As my voice narrated over his effort to walk with sincere emotion, it was everything I had ever wanted it to be.

True to form, again, Mr. Woods ran the documentary on every TV station he owned and the phones rang off the hook.

Dr. Walker, the director of Walker Institute, was so touched that she did something incredible. She wiped off their books all the additional charges Jack's family owed above what the insurance had paid. Looking back, I was so very grateful that God had given someone like me the ability to do this special with such far-reaching results. So many people called   Walker Institute after seeing this documentary to find out how they could get the help they needed. That was the best part.

Chapter Eight
The time between

It was really hard to see Tony Scott leave WTVY. Not only was I losing a co-host, but I was also losing a friend. Tony moved to a different market for awhile to become a part of a management team. He has now returned to Dothan where he and his wife Linda live right across the highway from us. We are still very close and Linda attends my ladies' Bible study.

Teresa Thomas had established a regular feature on our program while Tony was still my co-host, so the two of us had the program all alone for awhile. Teresa did Community Announcements and interviewed one guest on some upcoming event. Tom Nebel came in to do news and weather, and I did the rest of the features.

...

Before long, it was time to go back to the CBS Star Week-end. This time Jerry Vann was going to do the camera work. WTVY had worked out a great deal with our CBS affiliate in Columbus, Georgia. We did their taping for them, and they paid for our rooms. Jerry had to do double duty that year. Jerry Finn, production director at WTVY, and Sharon Enfinger in promotions also went with us to Atlanta.

I remember well the outstanding stars that year. Patrick Duffey had beautiful eyes and was an easy person to interview. He was a perfect choice for the good brother "Bobby" on *Dallas*. Lee Meriweather, a former "Miss America" who played Barnaby Jones's secretary on a very popular CBS detective show was one of the classiest ladies I had ever interviewed. She asked me if I liked the red in her hair. I told her it was perfectly beautiful. She explained that the director of *Barnaby Jones* had decided that lightening her hair with red would show up better on camera than her naturally dark brown hair. What else could I say? She was truly lovely with her reddened hair.

Ken Kercheval, "Cliff Barnes," in *Dallas* appeared to be a little sinister. Our interview went very well, but I was told by some of the other station personalities that he had been very difficult to interview. He also checked out early to go out on the town with a young woman he had just met and refused to finish the rest of his scheduled interviews. This did not go well with the CBS Executives.

Meeting Captain Kangaroo, wig and all, was a delight. Bob Keeshan was just as genuine and personable as he had appeared all those years on his "kiddy shows". It was like meeting a "living legend". We were all impressed with his friendly attitude.

Vic Tayback, "Mel" on *Alice*, had partied hard the night before he came to our suite the next morning to do our interview. Because he had previously seen some of our crew the night before, he removed his dark glasses long enough to ask me, "Say, did you and I have a good time last night?" It was evident that he wasn't sure. I had not been at the party, as I had gone to bed early. We all laughed at his comical remark.

Richard Dean Anderson of *McGiver* was very reserved. He was much more interested in the baseball game that was on TV than settling down for our interview. Nevertheless, we tore him away from the game to ask a few questions. I think he was, perhaps, really a little bit shy. Certainly, he was an devoted baseball fan!

Pernell Roberts and Greggory Harrison came in together. They were co-starring in CBS's new show, *Trapper John, M. D.*, a spin off from the very popular *Mash*. I had interviewed Greggory Harrison earlier when he was starring in *Logan's Run*, a short-lived futuristic TV show. If it had not been for Mr. Harrison, the interview would have been impossible. Pernell Roberts had lost a lot of weight, and he must have been desperately hungry, because he "growled" from the time he came into our room. No matter what I asked him, he didn't like it, and we had to start all over.

At Last, Greggory Harrison jumped in. "Aw, C'mon Pernell, don't be so difficult! Give this nice lady a break!"

It worked! He settled down (somewhat) until we completed the rest of the interview. Greggory Harrison was very willing to give us autographs, but we didn't bother to ask Mr. Roberts.

John Hillerman, "Higgins," on *Magnum P. I.*, was one of my favorite interviews. He was a talented individual in every way. Some of the visitors in our taping suite were "making fun" of the *Dukes of Hazzard*, and asked John Hillerman how he, as an actor, felt about the type of "good ol' boy" shows like the *Dukes*. I'll never forget how he answered. Without putting these people down who were questioning him, he stated, "Actually, I'm a fan! Whatever they do, somebody must like it. They sure have made a lot of money. I admire their success!"

When our taping was completed, I privately asked him if there was any way he could send me a "Magnum" hat. Wayne Register had urged me to ask him for one. Mr. Hillerman told me to give his assistant my address. (Weeks later, he sent me the hat accompanied with a sweet note. Wayne Register was so pleased to have his own "Magnum" hat.)

...

In expectation of great things to come, my son Trant planned to go with us to the CBS Star Week-end one summer. Because of all the stars he met, he wanted to be an actor for awhile. (Trant is an attorney in practice in Dothan today.)

The big stars that year were the following: Jack Elam (a great character actor from the old westerns) who was scheduled to star in a new CBS version of *Frankenstein*. He was to play the monster. When he came in for the interview, I knew we were in for a treat. We were not disappointed either. Just as I started the interview, he "pounced" on me, as if he were the monster attacking me. He simply would not get to the business at hand. He kept talking to my son Trant off camera, while I was diligently trying to conduct a proper interview. (Trant loved it!) Then, his good buddy David Ogden Steirs, (starring in "Mash" at the time, as the overly proper medical officer) sneaked into our bathroom and began "flushing our toilet". Just about the time I'd get Jack Elam to be a little serious, the toilet would flush again. This would send everyone into gales of laughter! I honestly don't remember if we ever did get a decent interview.

The next interview was with David Ogden Steirs. I knew it was coming, and it did! Right in the middle of my interview with him, Jack Elam walked over with a pair of scissors that he had found somewhere and cut David Ogden Steirs' tie off right at the top! So much for that interview. In spite of what this might imply, I do not believe they were intoxicated. They were just having loads of fun. They even apologized for "behaving badly" afterwards. They left our suite arm in arm laughing together as they went.

...

I totally misjudged Michael Keaton when I interviewed him. I thought he was nice enough, but I never thought he would make it as a star. Was I ever wrong! His CBS show, *Working Stiffs* did not make it, but as time passed, he has been a tremendous success in movies. He is still my favorite *Batman*.

That year, I thought James Stephens from *Paper Chase* would be a big star. Unfortunately, he hasn't been in too much since that show, which was, by the way, a story about law school.

Four of my very favorite interviews were with Susan Howard, who played the part of Ray Krebb's wife on *Dallas*; Sonny Shroyer, "Enos" on the *Dukes of Hazzard* (who later starred in a short-lived spin-off named *Enos*); Cooper Huckabee, a budding star on the CBS mini series, *The North and the South,* and Kevin Dobson from *Knott's Landing*.

Susan Howard and I hit it off immediately. She made no apologies about the fact that she was a dedicated

Christian.   Her career, she said, took a back seat in comparison with her relationship to God and her commitment to her family.

Sonny Shroyer, also a Christian, was a true Southern gentleman who chose to live near Valdosta, Georgia, rather than uproot his family and move them to Hollywood. He told me that if he made it as an actor that was fine, but if he didn't, that just wasn't God's perfect will for his life.

Cooper Huckabee walked into our taping suite dressed like a confederate soldier for his TV role in *The North and the South*. I had a Christian tract written by a real confederate soldier during a time of great testing during the civil war; therefore, just as we prepared to do the interview, I gave it to him. His response was immediate.

"I can't believe you're a Christian," he said excitedly, "I mean, I have just been praying for God to show me someone to share with my escort after I leave here today and here you are! I have just led him to Christ, and he needs to know more."

He then called the young man over to meet me (explaining what he had just told me). The young CBS escort just smiled. Then, I asked Cooper if - for any reason - he needed two Spanish New Testaments. (Remember the bibles Cliff Brannon had given me earlier? One whole box was in Spanish, so I had brought them along this year to give to all the kitchen help, maids and bell boys who spoke Spanish. I only had two bibles left.)

Well, Cooper had two Spanish speaking friends that had just come to Christ. He couldn't believe this turn of events.

Before long, my crew reminded me that we were running out of time. For that reason, I quickly started the interview. Patrick Swayze and James Reed were billed as the big stars of *The North and the South*, but to me, Cooper Huckabee was the only star I saw. No matter if he got killed in the mini series and may not have made it in Hollywood as an actor, wherever he is today, I know he is walking in God's perfect will for his life.

Kevin Dobson had played Telly Savales's sidekick in *Kojack* for years. When he came to do an interview with us, he was starring in the role of Michelle Lee's second husband on *Knotts Landing*, a spin-off from *Dallas*. I had been told earlier that he might not show up, since he had just received word that his father had to be rushed to the hospital for emergency surgery. When he came walking into our suite, I could tell that he was in a great deal of emotional pain. Feeling his hurt, I expressed to him my concern for his father and asked him if he minded if I prayed with him about his Dad.

"Would you?" he asked. So, I took his hand and prayed. When I finished, he thanked me over and over, as tears streamed down his face. Our interview went off without any problems. Subsequently, he put his arm around me and thanked me again. (By the way, his father pulled through the surgery.)

Esther Rolle, "Florida", on CBS's *Good Times*, was a surprise. She was very stiff and formal and refused to be addressed as "Florida." Her make-up man almost destroyed our interview. He kept telling us that our lights were bad. He put so much dark shadow on the star that it actually looked like "war paint." Our time was running out, consequently, we finally had to tell him we had to start the interview. She was very nice to me, but I was told that she had not been nice to other stations' personalities.

Larry Hagman, J. R., on *Dallas*, was a great interview. He kept on his big Texas hat and explained why he carried a miniature fan with him.

"I hate smoking," he almost growled, "so I keep this fan on to make sure the smoke from cigarettes won't blow on me."

When asked about his relationship to Patrick Duffy, he gave us an interesting tidbit of information.

"Everyone thinks I'm the weird one," Mr. Hagman explained, "Duffy is the real weirdo. He stands over in the corner on his head during our filming breaks chanting some Buddhist mumbo jumbo or other. Strange, strange guy!"

(Now whether this is true or not, I don't have a clue.)

Sarah Jessica Parker was a thirteen year old little girl when I interviewed her. (She is now a grown and very sexy lady.) Catherine Bach from the *Dukes of Hazzard* has a gorgeous figure but her skin is so deeply scarred from being overly exposed to the sun that we were startled at her looks up close. Gavin McLeod, who was on the *Mary Tyler Moore Show* at the time, and later played the Captain in *Love Boat* was, in reality, a very handsome man. Even though he was balding and gray, his skin was deeply tanned and smooth. His teeth were pearly white and his eyes were electric blue. What a pleasant surprise! I told him so!

"You are so handsome!" I said.

"Really?", he blushed.

Sharon Gless, "Cagney", and Tyne Daley, "Lacy", on *Cagney and Lacy* came in together. They kept brushing and re-brushing their hair and tugging and adjusting their sweaters. Sharon Gless wore a sunny yellow sweater while Ms Daley wore a pale blue one. They were both very nice to all of us and the interview went off smoothly.

...

At one of the annual CBS week-ends, Jerry Vann kept teasing me about my "brownie" camera. (He had a professional 35 m.m. camera.)

"Put that stupid camera up," he instructed. "It's embarrassing for you to take pictures of these folks with that little camera."

I fixed him, of course. At the end of the day, CBS sports anchor Phyllis George walked in. Jerry had been waiting all day to meet this beautiful former "Miss America". Not many women look as great as she does.

When it was time for pictures with Ms George, guess who was out of film? Jerry had to beg me to use my "brownie" camera to take his picture with Phyllis George. (The picture turned out great by the way.)

Jerry Vann also enjoyed needling me about Ed Asner's reaction when I welcomed him to our taping suite. Mr. Asner was starring in the TV series *Lou Grant*, about a big city newspaper editor, and he had lost quite a few pounds in preparation for the role.

Jerry's version is much better than mine as to what happened that day. Back at WTVY, Jerry would mimic the way I walked over to Mr. Asner. Then, he would intone in a high pitched real Southern voice. "Hello, Mr. Asner, I'm Ann Varnum from WTVY in Dothan, we're sooo glad to have you as our guest."

Finally, Jerry would almost fall out laughing as he related how Ed Asner took my hand and said, "Hot D---!" It was even funnier when Jerry demonstrated how this Southern lady reacted in shock. (I did not really react like he said, but I would have preferred a gentler greeting.)

...

President Ronald Reagan was coming to Dothan, and the entire city was filled with excitement. All the movie stars, TV stars, or country artists that I had ever met seemed pale in comparison to having the President of the United States visit our town. Every preparation was being made for his arrival.

The Dothan Civic Center could hold only a limited number of people; hence, every seat was coveted. Because I was part of the media, I got a seat. Was I excited!

Right before the date that the President was expected to arrive, City Commissioner S. A. Cherry came out to talk with me about all the preparations and plans for President Reagan's visit. Just as we were getting ready to go on the air, I suddenly remembered that I had not taken my vitamins that morning. I frantically rushed back to the water fountain, popped the pills in my mouth, swallowed quickly, and hurried back to "The Morning Show" set. I only had time to get my microphone on when Phillip Bump motioned, "You're on."

As I previewed the show and started my introduction of Mr. Cherry, a strange sensation came over me. I was beginning to feel very sick.. Hot water come up in my throat. My eyes began to water, and then, I knew what was about to happen. I tried in vain to motion to Phil to call for a break, but he couldn't understand what I was trying to tell him.

Mr. Cherry, on the other hand, kept trying to answer the first question I had asked him, while glancing nervously at me out of the corner of his eye. All at once, I yanked my microphone off, bolted off the set and made it to the lobby garbage can to throw up! Mr. Cherry didn't know what to do or say, so he just quit talking and stared into the camera. Finally, Director Joe Earl Holloway realized I had exited the set, and he went to a break. Moments later, embarrassed, I returned to my chair, put my microphone on and apologized to Mr. Cherry. The commercial break ended, and we were back on. We never said a word about why I had left the set, but everywhere I went for weeks afterwards, I got asked, "What happened?" Now, Jerry Vann had something else to kid me about.

"Can't you act right just once?" he would ask. "I can't believe you actually threw up on the air! Just too much partying at night, I guess."

When the big day arrived. Ricky Harper and I left for downtown Dothan immediately after the "Morning Show." John Williams anchored from WTVY and Chris Bence acted as Master of Ceremonies at the Civic Center. We covered everything live. Our TV reporters did an excellent job commenting along the way as the President was being escorted into town. By the time President Reagan walked into the Civic Center wearing a very dashing off-white suit, I literally felt that my heart would burst with pride. The cheers were deafening. He sat very close to us and ate, with relish, his country style meal.

I never did get to meet President Reagan personally or interview him, but I did catch a quick interview with another very special person that day - Senator Jeremiah Denton. It was a day in my life I will never forget.

...

Due to WTVY having purchased some great new equipment, it was now possible for me to do a lot more things "live" on location instead of having to tape every segment to be replayed later. Doing a live remote can be very tricky. Not only does the equipment have to work right, but the interviews have to be done entirely different.

When we shot a TV show from Panama City Beach, it was usually done out-of- doors. If it rained, we had to quickly move to another location. Once, when we started the show, the steam fogged up all our cameras. Another time, just as I opened the show from the Indian Summer Seafood Festival Fairgrounds, the remote van blew a gasket, and we were "off the air". I'm so glad that I had left back up tapes for Teresa Thomas to use at WTVY in case of just such an event.

...

The city of Bonifay, Florida, invited us to come to their city to do one of their big parades live. I co-hosted the event with a local celebrity who later was found murdered.

Right in the middle of the parade, I looked up and saw an airplane being towed down the street. There was no way it could pass by the platform that we had set up for our cameras. Recognizing the problem, I had to explain - as best I could - the situation to our production crew without being on camera. I had one eye on our TV monitor, while I was standing up to notify the crew up above me. Reading my signals, they spotted the difficulty just in time to stop the plane. It had to be backed all the way in reverse to the first place where it could be turned off to a side street. We would have certainly experienced a disaster if we had not been able to see what was about to happen in time.

The grand marshal of the parade was one of the astronauts. He joined me on the platform after he opened the parade. My dilemma was that no one had told me his name or what mission he had worked on. The local man who was my co-host shrugged his shoulders when I questioned him and moved out of the way. There was so much crowd noise that the astronaut could hardly hear me. I couldn't speak any louder because our viewers would have been blasted by my voice. It was certainly an interesting situation. I don't think he ever realized that I didn't know who he was. I had a script for the parade all right, but at the beginning of the format, all that was written was: Grand Marshal: Astronaut.

...

The energetic Pat Elliot invited me to cover the annual Older American's Day at the Dothan Civic Center. It became one of the yearly programs that I did every May. These senior citizens are so wonderful. One year Mrs. Senior Alabama came and performed an animated hula dance. She was in great shape for someone her age. WTVY's viewers enjoy the cloggers, western line dancers and singers that appear every time we host the event. I'm convinced that senior adults must get an extra shot of adrenaline when they turn sixty-five.

...

When Wiregrass Commons Mall opened, we did a "Morning Show" from a marvelous dinosaur exhibit. The motorized dinosaur made real spooky noises and appeared life - like in every way. People flocked to the mall to see this educational display.

Another show that we always try to do live is the Arts and Crafts Show hosted by Jimmy and Jackie Patterson at Wiregrass Commons. Meeting genuine artisans from all over the country is exciting. I have also developed close friendships with our repeat guests. One year, I donned a fuchsia ribbon wig just as we closed the show. The lady who made those wigs was completely sold out by lunch time. Another time, I wore a turquoise Indian necklace which sold for around $1,500.00. They sold three of them during their craft show. TV is a great seller!

...

Art Linkletter came to town to so a special for senior Americans at Wiregrass Commons Mall. I was invited to do our program with him that morning. If there has ever been a polished spokesperson, it is Art Linkletter. He inspired everyone, as well as shared some of the most practical advice for anyone sixty plus. I was fascinated. (I only wish he had asked me what I had in my purse. I had packed my boiled egg and my girdle that day just in case. Just a little humor here. Remember his program where he asked the audience what they had in their purses? He gave cash prizes for strange items not usually carried in a woman's purse.)

...

One person I could never forget was Richard Simmons. Our crew set up early at Wiregrass Commons where Mr. Simmons was to appear, and I was there earlier than usual myself. All at once, I heard this really loud voice yelling my name from way down the mall. "Ann, Ann, where are you?"

It was Richard Simmons, of course. Suddenly, he burst in, ran up on the stage that we had made, picked me up and began spinning me round and round yelling, "Ann, Ann, I've found you! I've found you!"

By the time he put me down, I was really dizzy and out of breath! I knew I was in for a wild show. It was probably one of the best shows I have ever done. I never knew from one moment to the next what was going to happen. I had arranged to have a huge salad put out for Richard Simmons to demonstrate his newest low calorie, fat free salad dressings. Instead of what I had planned, he began wearing the salad. He put cucumbers over his eyes, a carrot in his teeth, one vegetable behind his ears and on and on. We also showed some of his videos, "Sweatin to the Oldies" to assist people who want to lose weight.

Whatever you may think of Mr. Simmons, he really is a fun person, and he is very sincere about helping overweight people get in shape. Our switchboard was jammed with calls about his weight loss program.

...

Bonifay, Florida is still one of my favorite cities to visit. For years, I have been invited to do our show there live during the annual Kiwanis Club Rodeo. It is truly a classic event like our National Peanut Festival. Sandy Spears and Joan Manuel Holman have become two of my dearest friends as a result of all their efforts to coordinate our broadcasts each year.

The Bonifay Junior Woman's Club always prepared a very special reception for our WTVY crew, usually at their clubhouse, or at Blitch's Restaurant. The rodeo cowboys were truly entertaining, and the clowns sometimes risked their lives to protect these bull riders when a bull threw them.

On one occasion, I got to ride a horse into the stadium to open the show. The owner had told me that her horse had a very sore mouth, so she asked me not to pull too tightly on the reins. Being a tender-hearted person, I was too easy with the horse. She almost got away from me. I couldn't even slow her down in order to do the proper opening for the show. (I had to endure more funny jokes about this.)

Chapter Nine
Tom Nebel joins me and Teresa Thomas on "The Morning Show"

When WTVY management decided to have Tom Nebel join me as a co-host, I welcomed him. Up until this time, I had been doing all the interviews myself. In my opinion, a male and female team always adds a special dimension to a talk show. Tom was young, energetic and very nice looking. His style was completely casual, and even, a little restrained. Immediately, our viewers loved him.

Tom not only continued doing our news and weather segments, but he opened the program with me and joined me for as many interviews as he could. Once a lady brought her pet boa constrictor to our show. Brave Tom wrapped the snake around his neck. I even got up the nerve to touch it!

Due to this particular episode, one of Tom Nebel's fans called to say, "I sure do love you, Tom, but hands that touch snakes will never hold mine!" Tom got a big kick out of this.

I received a kit in the mail on how to make chocolate candy pops with an individual's personal picture stamped on it. Tom and I decided to try it on TV. We had to make pictures of each of us, send them back to the company, and then wait until they could send the prints back. Out next move was to put our picture on the candy pops.

When we had all our props together, we decided to tape the demonstration. While Tom was heating up the chocolate, Teresa was getting the pop sticks ready to place in the molds. I noticed that Tom was about to splatter chocolate on his nice white shirt; hence, I tried to put an apron on him. In my rush, I got the ties that were supposed to go around his neck and tied one of them down to the tie that should go around his waist. Realizing my mistake, I tried to undo the ties. I was jerking Tom around, and he was really getting tickled at me. Our cameraman moved to the side to catch me trying to untie the apron instead of focusing in on what Tom and Teresa were doing with the candy.

Needless to say, the demonstration was much funnier than we had planned. The candy, nevertheless, turned out to be delicious, and our images were on each pop. To top it all off, we were requested to send all out bloopers to a TV show in England called, *It'll Be All Right on the Night*. We sent the "candy making tape" to them, and they aired it on British TV.

Becky Ledenham Copeland had hosted a kiddie cartoon show as "Miss Becky" for a number of years. The children were not the only ones who watched the "Miss Becky" show - the men loved it, too! Becky got as much teasing from Jerry Vann as I did. When it was time for the show to end, Becky continued to work in the bookkeeping department as she had always done.

Subsequently, she added promotions to her job title. She, Judy Calhoun, and Ann Adams, two of our sales ladies, did WTVY's decorating. They re-did our station condominiums in Panama City, and later, as a surprise to

Mr. Woods, directed all of us as we re-did the old WTVY building just in time for a visit by Mr. Woods' bankers. To be truthful, we almost completed the job overnight. We have always had a strong bond between employees at WTVY - just like a family.

One of the funniest events that happened to me at WTVY was the day I had a very strange visitor in my office. Ann Adams had come in to tell me something when I looked up and saw, entering my doorway, a huge pig! I remember saying, "Don't look now, Ann, but a pig has just followed you in."

She yelled when she saw the animal and jumped in my chair. The huge pig ran behind my desk and wedged himself (or herself) between the wall and my tapes. Acting curious, the poor beast started rooting through my stacks of recipes. Gene Ragan was not far behind. Taking his hat off, he began apologizing for the pig invading my office. "Don't touch it," Gene admonished. "He might hurt you!"

I really wasn't afraid of the pig, and by this time, I was scratching him on his head. Momentarily, Gene and the animal's owner was able to somehow get the pig out of my office and back to the trailer which he had escaped from.

Jerry Vann told everyone that the pig came to see me for counseling because he didn't want to wind up "a Frosty Morn" ham!

Very soon after the pig's visit, another "critter" found his way into my office. I was talking with one of the D. J. 's from WTVY-FM when a beautiful mallard duck wandered into my office. It was obvious that it was "dazed". Susan Tatom, our head copywriter, who was also another animal lover, tried to catch it to see if it was injured. This undertaking was impossible because the duck turned and ran back down the hall and started flying as soon as he got outside the open door. Susan followed for a short distance until she almost tripped over a mama cat who had just delivered a litter of kittens.

Susan hadn't been able to help the mallard (who had probably flown into one of our t.v. tower's guide wires and had become disoriented), but she was able to care for the cat and her kittens. We took them in and made sure they were all properly fed and looked after.

...

In those days, we did everything in our big studio. Gene Ragan had his farm animals on, and I had no problem bringing all types of pets in for our show. Once, we featured a huge steer named "Slim Jim" on our program. He got a little nervous and left us a huge mess to clean up later. Another time, a similar steer got away from his owner and nearly kicked our studio door down.

...

T. G. McGinty's had opened in Dothan and the owner, John Cox, wanted Gene Ragan, Red Holland and me to do a commercial together for his restaurant. Gene talked about the great steaks from the middle of a pasture full of cows, Red bragged on the great seafood while he was seen in the center of a swimming pool. To end the spot, I was shown at the cash register discussing the great service at T. G. McGinty's. Everyone who has ever watched our show knew that my dog Boone had been missing for some time; therefore, John thought it would be great for me to ask the guest who was pretending to pay his check, "Have you seen my dog, Boone?"

We may not have helped the restaurant's business, but the commercial was a favorite around town. (Before long, I did find "Boone" in Samson, Alabama some 50 miles from Dothan.)

Tom Nebel and I began co-hosting the "Little Miss National Peanut Festival Pageant" about the same time that we started working together on the *Morning Show*. We have shared some memorable experiences during our time as pageant M. C.'s. Listening to all the great conversations from the little queens has been particularly amusing. Something not quite so funny happened during one of the pageants when I almost slipped off the stool I was sitting on. It was a miracle that I was able to catch myself before I fell. I could have been seriously hurt had I fallen, or perhaps, even worse, shown much more of myself than I ever would have wanted to show.

Another event that Tom and I co-hosted together annually was the National Peanut Festival Parade. Each time we would try to correct the problems that we had experienced from the previous year. For many years, David Ethridge from "D' Ethridge" has provided us with "his" and "her" furs to wear during the parade. Some years, in contrast to the cold, the weather turned unseasonably hot, and we hosted the parade in the heat. One year, we almost got rained out. That was the time our TV production team put a cover over us, and, as it continued to pour, the rain began to fill up the canopy. One of our cameramen put a hole in the canvas to keep it from collapsing on us. Because of this, the rain water began to gush out between us and the camera. It was necessary to move in order to continue.

Good fortune turned bad one year when the parade was completely rained out. Every queen, float and band was soaked. My heart went out to all the people who had worked so very hard to put together this tremendous event.

...

On account of our WTVY anniversary celebrations, Tom Nebel and I welcomed back to the "Morning Show" many of the on air personalities that had moved on to other things. For the entire month of February that year, we interviewed everyone from former talk show hostesses to those individuals who had previously worked in news. We also included many of our present employees who had been around since the early days.

Bonnie Buckner was the very first lady to host programming at WTVY. She provided some wonderful film clips while explaining, how, in the early days, TV 4 had just literally stayed "live" all day. Back then when television was so new, people would watch almost anything. "Once", she said, "Joe Holloway (not our Joe Earl) and I set up in downtown Dothan near the Old Bauman's building. We talked all morning to anyone who would talk to us!"

Next, John Gause shared some great stories of his early "on air" commercials.

"I did a commercial for Bauman's one morning", he explained, "It was on the new easy - to- use Polaroid camera. As I demonstrated the technique, I snapped the picture, pulled the print out to show how easy it was to operate, and the whole roll came out! I think I said something like - 'well, it is easy for most everyone'!"

"Another time", John continued, "I tried to demonstrate the latest frost-free refrigerator. I went over to try to open the door, and it wouldn't open! Barbara Gellersted then walked over and opened it without any difficulty. That was really embarrassing."

"And, of course," he added, "everyone thought that Betty Gault and I were married. I guess it was because we worked together and our names are so similar - Gause and Gaut. George, Betty's husband, often threatened to send her bills to me."

Barbara Gellersted Adams was just as cute and petite as ever. She is a real talker, just like I am. We both laughed as she told how she behaved during her first interview with a big television star. (It was some host of a TV game show.)

"The more nervous I got, the faster I talked," she giggled, "I don't think the poor man got to say much of anything."

Betty Gault visited us also to share the stories of hosting the "Morning Show" with Bob Peterman and Bob Howell. Bob Hacker would also come in and play the organ for the show. (It was truly the Betty, Bob, Bob, and Bob show then.)

One of Betty's most memorable experiences was the time she drove over to Georgia to interview David Jansen (who starred in *The Fugitive* on CBS) during the filming of *The Green Berets*. She told us that they were so excited about getting to meet David Jansen that they didn't even consider trying to interview John Wayne.

Laurie Lynn Benson Morris hosted an afternoon program on WTVY for awhile. She laughed as she related her experience of doing a live commercial and having a prop fall on her head which almost knocked her out. She even got to show her new engagement ring on TV during her stint as a TV hostess.

Gene Ragan later told us that both he and Laurie Lynn had been single at the time they had worked together.

"I was really disappointed when Laurie Lynn got engaged," he smiled. "That surely shut the door for me."

Kenneth Hicks came back to explain how he had become "the dancing cameraman".

"One morning," he related, "we had some peppy music playing as we went off the air, so I just started doing a little shuffle. The other cameraman threw the camera on me until we ended the show. We really started something then because the viewers began calling to request that I dance again. Because of this, I brushed up on my dancing and that's how we ended the show each day from then on."

Tom and I asked Kenneth to dance for us right then and there, and he did. We had some great rock and roll music to close the show that day. (The ony time we could have added a cameraman's performance occurred when Henry Nance attempted to imitate the gymnasts we had previously had on that day. The other cameraman, Phil Bump, threw the camera over on him until poor Henry split his pants! That ended the saga of the gymnast cameraman.)

Bob Peterman returned to tell us how he got the job at WTVY and wound up hosting the "Morning Show' with Betty Gaut. Bob had been through some really serious health problems and ultimately had to take early retirement. The day he visited us, though, he really looked good. (That was probably the last TV show that Bob ever did because he died a short time later. In a special memorial to Bob, we re-played that interview.)

Wayne Powell, a former news anchor, came to tell us he now owned his own bait and tackle shop in Georgia.

Preston T., the former teenage dance show host, also had experienced some serious health problems. At the present time, he manages a cemetery. John Williams returned from Florida to visit us that year on our anniversary. (We're so glad he decided to return to WTVY.)

...

On January 15, 1987, while Tom Nebel was still doing the show with me, all my former co-hosts planned a very special birthday celebration for me. Chris Bence had the idea and put it together. Bob Howell and Rex Roach couldn't be there in person so instead, they made a video tape to air that morning. Chris, Don Day and Tony Scott showed up in person. I was so overcome with emotion that I couldn't say anything. I just hugged them all. It was one of the happiest days of my life. It may be hard to believe, but I never had one cross word with a single one of my co-hosts. Each one was totally different in personality and temperament, but I can truthfully say I love them all. We are still dear friends to this day.

One of the regular features on the "Morning Show" during the late 80's was "Focus on Aging." I selected inspirational seniors who were 90 years old or older and interviewed them concerning the secrets of their long lives. One morning a woman called and practically insisted that I have her mother on the program. For some reason, a little "red flag" went up while I was talking with her. I asked the usual questions and this person assured me that her mother would have no problem coming to do the show early in the morning.

When the scheduled day arrived, the little old lady could hardly manage to make it to our studio. She was assisted by a walker and her daughter, but it was still hard for her to walk. It was very obvious that being on the "Morning Show" was not her idea at all.

By the time we got her seated, it was almost time to open the show. Phillip Bump, our cameraman, tried politely to get the lady to take her baseball cap off. He explained that the cap would keep viewers from seeing her face. She absolutely refused to remove it!

Right after that, we were on. I started my regular introduction when I heard - what I feared I was hearing - the dear woman was snoring. I just kept talking into the camera about why we did " Focus on Aging" etc. until I could think of what to do. Finally, I motioned to her daughter whose name I could not remember.

"Ma'am," I pleaded, "would you like to tell your mother it's time for the interview?"

The woman got the message, came over and shook her mother who sputtered, "Is someone talking to me?"

To say that the interview was a difficult one is an understatement. The highlight of our visit came when I asked her, "To what do you attribute your long life?" When she didn't understand this, I re-phrased my question, "Why do you think you have managed to live this long?"

She blurted out then, "I don't know why I'm still here, I've been waiting to die for a long time!"

Well, that ended that. I had no choice but to thank her and close out the interview. We caught flack about this show for weeks!

...

Congressman Bill Dickenson made regular visits to the "Morning Show" to keep us informed of legislation affecting our area. When he was running for re-election one year, he visited us on location during the live coverage of the National Peanut Festival.

Billy Joe Camp, who was the Democratic contender for Dickenson's job, called to also request a guest appearance. The day he was set to appear on the program, our TV production crew had placed the cameras in the barn where the prized chickens were housed. Just as we started the interview with Mr. Camp, for some reason, the chickens began squawking with all their might. I couldn't hear Mr. Camp, and he surely couldn't hear me. We had to call for a break in order to hurriedly change locations. Live TV is never boring!

...

The gifted Pastor, D. James Kennedy, made a guest appearance on our television show while he was in our area. Afterwards, on his national television program, he mentioned having been on our station. My mother happened to be watching Dr. Kennedy that particular morning and was so excited to hear his kind remarks about her daughter.

...

Harold Bredesen was undergoing treatment at Sealey Springs in Cottonwood, Alabama. I had previously met him in Opelika, Al when I was invited by Mrs. Fob James to meet him at a Christian Women's conference. Rev. Bredesen had been responsible for helping many

Hollywood stars get their lives back on track, including actor and singer Pat Boone.

When I went to do an interview with Rev. Bredesen, he had John de Lorean, the famous auto maker with him. (One of his famous cars was used in the *Back to the Future* series starring Michael J. Fox.) Not only did we get to interview Rev. Bredesen about all his efforts to work toward peace with middle eastern countries, but we got to interview Mr. DeLorean as well.

John DeLorean had lost his financial empire about the time his marriage had ended in divorce.

"Both of these experiences were devastating," he shared, "but thanks to caring friends like Harold Bredesen, I now have a personal relationship with Jesus Christ. My life is radically changed."

...

David and Tawanna Hays got the surprise of their lives when they discovered they were expecting triplets. The biggest shock came, later, when the babies were born and there were four instead of just three.

Joe Earl Holloway and I traveled to my hometown of Geneva, Al, to interview the Hays family. It was quite an experience. The two boys were identical and so were the two girls. Their mother, Tawanna, told us that she put red fingernail polish on one of the boy's toes and one of the girls toes, in order to keep them apart.

While we were there, David was busy making formula because two of the four had started fussing. My mother, Elizabeth Jones, had come along to watch us; therefore, she wound up holding one baby for us. When all of the babies started crying, it became even more fun!

Through the years, the Hays quadruplets have visited our show many times. On one of their birthdays, we had a big sheet cake for them to help celebrate. One boy and one girl, who were the extroverts, dived right in, while the other two remained seemingly uninterested. The entire wiregrass area has enjoyed watching the quadruplets grow up.

...

J. D Sumner, lead singer for the Stamps, who for years backed up Elvis Presley, first came to our program with Jimmy and Jackie Patterson's Arts and Crafts Show. He has been a regular guest and friend ever since. Telling "Elvis" stories is one of his specialties. His deep voice is also listed as the world's deepest voice in the *Guiness Book of World Records.*

One of my favorite stories that J. D. told, was the time Elvis pretended that his life had been threatened. Elvis later arranged to have someone shoot off some blanks in order to play a joke on his musicians. J. D. said that he threw himself over Elvis when he heard the shots in order to protect him. It was funny to Elvis but not to J. D.

"Another time," J. D. laughed, "Elvis deliberately set off the fire alarm in the hotel where we were staying. The sprinklers came on and we were drenched!" (Of course, Elvis paid for all the damages caused by this practical joke.)

...

For many years, Charles Woods hosted an annual Premier Party Night right before the opening of the new

CBS season. Tom Nebel acted as Master of Ceremonies for the big event while I did interviews with our special guests. Kim Zimmer, "Reva Shayne" on *The Guiding Light* was one of our featured stars. She was as friendly as anyone we've ever interviewed. No wonder she stays on top! I talked with her at length about her concern for her toddler's day care in New York. (It was during the time of the sex abuse charges leveled against workers in a day care center which had made National headlines.) Kim Zimmer, as a career lady, wanted to be sure that her daughter would receive the proper care while she was at work.

Steven Ford attended our Premier Party one year. He was the son of former President Gerald Ford. Not only did Mr. Ford talk to us about what it was like to be the son of the President of the United States, but, he freely discussed his mother's struggle to overcome drug problems. He expressed pride that she had openly admitted her addiction, and consequently, had spearheaded the opening of the Betty Ford Treatment Center for Drug and Alcohol Abuse. Steven Ford's real passion, he told us, was raising thoroughbred horses.

...

Dack Rambo was starring in *Dallas* when he was invited to be our honored guest at the annual premier party. Scott Griffin, who was the producer of our "Morning Show" at the time, accompanied me to pick up Mr. Rambo. We had a big stretch limousine waiting for him at the Montgomery airport when he arrived by plane. When he joined us at the curb, I thought we were in for yet another "strange star". He was dressed in ragged, faded jeans, a weathered blue denim shirt, and had a blue bandanna tied around his head like a sweat band.

Scott and I changed out mind about Dack Rambo as soon as he started talking to us on the way back to Dothan. We genuinely liked him! He said I reminded him of his favorite aunt who was a sweet Southern lady. He even told us how Loretta Young had discovered him and his identical twin brother, Dirk, at church one Sunday. Both boys were cast as her sons in her television show after then.

One of the saddest moments of his life, he confided in us, was when his twin brother Dirk was tragically burned to death in a car wreck. Dack's emotions were at the surface as he shared this with us. He explained how twins, especially identical ones, often feel what the other twin is experiencing. The rest of his story was pretty graphic, and Scott and I were both moved to compassion for his loss.

While Dack Rambo poured out his heart to us, it was a perfect opportunity for me to share how my faith in God had seen me through the toughest times in my own life. Scott spoke up, as well, to say that the only peace he had ever experienced in his life was when he was totally walking with God.

All the way from Montgomery we talked to this very troubled young man. When we arrived at his motel in Dothan, he asked us if we would please stay and have dinner with him. I then called my husband, Jerome, to come over to join us and meet Dack.

We spent hours sharing with Dack Rambo. He was visibly moved as he told us how he had always had a healthy respect for religion, but had never understood that someone could have a personal relationship with God like we described. We finally had to say "goodnight" so that we could get some rest before the next night's big event.

The entire week-end was a great success. Dack looked and dressed like the star that he was at our premier party. The women flocked to him and everyone wanted his autograph.

Even after Dack Rambo returned to Hollywood he continued to call us for a long time. According to reports, he later admitted that he had been a bisexual before turning his life over to Christ. I saw Dack on a number of both secular and Christian television programs as he shared his testimony about how he got saved. Dack ultimately died of aids. I sincerely hope his conversion was genuine.

We had tried, in vain, to call him shortly before his death, but his phone number had been changed.

...

John Gause, WTVY's sales manager, called me one day while I was covering an agricultural story with Gene Ragan.

"Ann," John said, " How would you like to fly to Nashville tomorrow and attend *Fanfare* as a special guest of the Oak Ridge Boys? Their agent thinks if you did some interviews with them up there it might help sales for their Ozark Civic Center Show next month."

I thought about it - half a second - and agreed to go. The next morning off I flew to Nashville, not knowing what to expect. I was met at the airport by a nice lady who worked for the Oak Ridge Boys. She took me miles out in the country and left me at a new condo development. I didn't see another person until she picked me up early the next morning.

Again, I had to work with a different camera crew from my own. They were extremely nice to me, and so were the Oak Ridge Boys. We decided to do a few short interviews before we left for *Fanfare*. I'm glad we did, because from then on we were plunged into the wildest time I had ever experienced.

As we exited the door to the big hotel leading to *Fanfare*, I was startled at the crowd that was pushing and yelling for their favorite singers. All at once, the Oaks were swallowed up in the crowd, and so was I. It seemed that we were being crushed from every side. People were behaving like crazed teenagers. After some trying moments, we finally pushed our way back to the *Fanfare* show stage. I was already exhausted by then, and my lavender suit was rumpled and stained. (Someone spilled their drink on me.)

When the show started, it was everything a country fan could have dreamed of. Star after star appeared with their own unique style of country music. One of my favorite performers, Lee Greenwood, really pleased the fans with "God Bless the USA," and then really brought down the house with his great saxophone playing! When he finally finished, he got a thunderous applause. As he left the stage he came right past me, smiled and said, "Hello". Now whether he had any idea of who I was, I don't know. I had already interviewed him previously on two different occasions. Mr. Greenwood had always been a very polite star who did great interviews.

In the middle of the show, the Oak Ridge Boys performed. The crowd went wild over them! I was so tired, but there was still more interviews to do.

After *Fanfare*, we got all our taping done, and I was on my way back to my condo. The Oak Ridge Boys had been wonderful to me, and I featured them for a week on our "Morning Show." (By the way, they played to a sell -

out crowd the next month at the Ozark Civic Center. I hope our interviews helped.)

...

Benji Clark had been kept as a virtual prisoner by her abusive father from the time she had been eleven years old. He not only sexually and physically abused her, but he nailed all the windows shut and kept the doors locked in their house. She lived in terror. Benji had watched him stomp her helpless, pregnant mother to death. He was never prosecuted. Her two brothers had run away, but she was too young to escape.

Then one day, a Sunday School teacher came by her terrible little prison. Benji had gone to Sunday School only a few times in her life before her mother died, but her name was still on the Sunday School roll; consequently, the teacher had come to visit her.

In those early days, the welfare department had no authority to forcibly take a child out of a home. When the teacher heard about Benji's terrible plight, the kind lady made a plan of escape for Benji. That night, when her father came home, Benji rushed past him in the dark and ran as fast as she could to the place where the teacher had arranged to meet her. For years the young girl had nightmares of her father screaming profanities at her. There was a lot more to her story, of course, but time doesn't permit us to tell it now. By the time Benji appeared on our program, she had become a counselor who worked with sexually abused children.

"I can tell those kids, they, too, can make it. I did!," Benji concluded.

...

Mary Kay Beard had been on the FBI 's most wanted list for months when she was apprehended in Birmingham, AL. For over seven years, she had worked as a burglar robbing banks. Her ex - husband had taught her the trade. When he deserted her, she continued without him. Mary Kay was also in trouble with the underworld because she worked as an independent who refused to pay any percentage to the mob bosses.

Of all the places for her to be caught, Birmingham, Al was the least likely.

Mary Kay (who looked like a gentle school teacher, ironically) went on to tell us that it had been her mother's prayers that had caused her to be stopped. Due to the Birmingham City Jail's policy of allowing Christians to come in to witness and bring bibles to inmates, Mary Kay had been given a new bible. In her boredom, she started reading.

God used a very unusual scripture to change her heart. It was found in Ezekiel 36:26, "A new heart will I give you, and a new spirit will I put within you. And I will take away the stony heart out of your flesh and give you a heart of flesh."

After her own conversion, her first convert was the large black inmate that Mary Kay had often violently fought with. When they were transferred to Julia Tutwiler Prison, the two women formed a bible study group. In the ensuing months, they requested that they be allowed to be baptized. Subsequently, two guards handcuffed them, took them to a nearby church and went into the baptismal pool with them.

Just because Mary Kay and her friend had become Christians did not mean that they got shorter sentences. In fact, they never asked for any special favors. Today, both women are out of prison. Mary Kay and her new husband have a half - way house for inmates who have just been released from prison. Truly, Mary Kay has a new heart.

...

Meeting Dr. Michael De Bakey, a pioneer in heart transplantation surgery, was one of the biggest highlights in my career. I was surprised at the softness of his huge hands. He told me how the transplantation program had started, related some of the stories of the first trials, and ended his remarks with the fact that he believed heart transplants would be almost routine one day.

...

Vicki Love was a very popular Dothan resident who needed a heart transplant. Her parents, Gerald and Sara Love, appealed to the entire community for help, and they got it. Everyone rallied around Vicki. She got her new heart just in time, as she was very close to death when the call came that the needed organ had been located. I had the privilege of interviewing her before and after her heart transplant. (More than then years have passed since Vicki got her new heart. She has been an inspiration to us all.)

...

Dr. Andreas Gruentzig was the doctor who developed angioplasty (the balloon catheter used to open arteries.) I interviewed him at the Southeast Alabama Medical Center before he was to speak at a physicians meeting. I spent nearly three hours with this dedicated man who had done so very much to help save lives.

Dr. Gruentzig was a very tall, handsome man with a wonderful sense of humor. He told me about being ridiculed by his other medical associates when he told them what he was working on.

"I got the idea, actually," he told me, "from my plumber who asked me why I couldn't just ream out his arteries like he unplugged my toilet."

"Then", he stated, "when I brought my presentation to the United States Medical Association, I was out jogging on the beach before the meeting and was asked about my project by a U. S. reporter. I told him about everything I had developed."

"Later," he concluded, "I found out that I had been interviewed by a reporter from *The National Inquirer*. You can just imagine how they reported it. They simply drew a diagram on a partially nude woman to explain what angioplasty was. I had to live that one down, too," he laughed.

At this time, angioplasty is a medical technique used by the very same doctors who once scoffed at Dr. Gruentzig 's ideas.

Tragically, Dr. Andreas Gruentzig and his wife were killed in an airplane crash near Atlanta a very short time after my interview. Dr. Gruentzig had his own plane and failed to heed the warning of the air traffic controllers who urged him not to continue his flight in a storm. Speculation was that Dr. Gruentzig had relied on his sophisticated equipment to see him through. (What a tremendous loss to medical science.)

...

A few weeks after I met Dr. Gruentzig, I interviewed two local cardiologists, Dr. Allan Schwadron and his partner, Dr. Luther McEachern. Both of these young doctors were quite knowledgeable and impressive. Two weeks after our show aired, Dr. McEachern was killed in a freak motorcycle accident.

(It was, again, a great loss for medicine.)

...

Tom Nebel could play along with almost any scenario presented to him. He enjoyed the costumed characters that visited us as much as I did. We interviewed celebrity mascots such as "Winnie the Pooh," "Aqua Duck" from Water World, "McGruff," the crime fighting dog, "Billy Bob", from a local pizza place and story book characters from area craft shows. We even visited with Elsie the cow, from Borden's Milk company. (She was a real cow!) Having a co-host like Tom was always a plus.

In my line of work, I know change is inevitable. Soon, Tom Nebel was moved to the night time weather spot, and Gary Bruce was transferred to mornings to work with me and Teresa Thomas.

Chapter Ten
Gary Bruce, the total professional, co-hosts "The Morning Show" with me

Gary Bruce is an excellent weatherman. He is also a gifted writer and producer. One thing I learned very quickly about Gary is his strong desire to accomplish his work in a timely manner. At first after Gary was switched to "mornings", I don't think he was interested in participating in our interviews. He did his news and weather segments every day on the program without much interaction with me or Teresa in the beginning.

It was during this period in our show's history, that I was invited to go to Atlanta to tape Dr. Robert Marmer's radial kerototomy surgery. Dr. Marmer was an early pioneer in this new technique used to correct near-sightedness . Wayne Register and I had to dress in surgical scrubs in order to do our video and interviews. The patient was Dottie Snider, the female coach of Kentucky 's "Lady Wildcat" basketball team. In those days, one eye was done at a time. After the first eye was well, then the second eye was adjusted.

When we arrived, Dottie Snider had already had surgery on the first eye. When we asked her what she thought about her treatment, she excitedly said,

"I was utterly amazed!", she exclaimed, "The very next morning after surgery on this first eye, I could read the cereal box across the table!"

I asked her about pain and she answered, "I have experienced some very scratchy feelings in my eye but no real pain."

Dr. Marmer then prepared us for what he was going to do next. In a few minutes, Dottie was lying down on his surgical table. Clamps to hold her upper and lower eyelids open were put into place, and drops were administered to deaden her eye. Then, Dr. Marner started his surgery. It consisted of making calculated cuts on the eye in order to correct the degree of near-sightedness. She didn't appear to be in pain, but Wayne and I both began to feel nauseated. It was very warm in the little room, and I guess watching someone operate directly on another person's eye was a little more than we could handle.

No matter what, we knew we had to continue. He was talking us through the process as he did it; therefore, we had to get it the first time. There could be no "second take." Everything turned out rather well. At their request, Wayne made Dr. Marmer and Dottie Snider copies of the tape on her surgery.

When it was aired on early morning TV, our viewers were pleased at how well we had focused in on the eye. Some, nevertheless, complained about our showing the actual surgery during the breakfast hour.

After much preparation, Dr. Martin Margolies and Dr. Jimmy Carter began doing R. K. in Dothan, I invited them to be on our program to talk further about this technique to improve eyesight. The surgery had progressed even further than when Wayne and I videotaped the procedure with Dr. Marmer.

At the time, I had just started wearing glasses to drive, but my close vision was fine. After hearing about my need for glasses, Dr. Carter asked me to come out to his office to see if I would be a candidate for R. K. I was, and he offered to do the surgery for me.

The day Phillip Bump and I drove out to tape the R.K. surgery, I confided in Phil that I didn't think I could interview Dr. Carter while I was being operated on. Phil laughed. We decided to go with video only.

I guess I trusted Dr. Carter so much that I refused to take the usual valium which is given to patients before surgery. He had already assured me that the drops he used in my eyes would deaden any feelings. As the camera rolled, I watched Dr. Carter do the surgery. It seemed like he was "stroking my eye" with a hair. There was hardly any discomfort. Next, he did the second eye. It was over before I knew it.

Phil held up pretty well and did an excellent job on the video. My daughter Paige took me home where I took the usual sleeping pills. When I woke up later, I could see so well that I recognized the ducks on the other side of the pond! I was in no pain at all.

The next month, when Dr. Carter came out to our program to talk over our video, I surprised him with a musical opening to his interview. I played "I Can See Clearly Now - the rain is gone!" by Johnny Nash. He really seemed to like this added touch.

The second surgery we videotaped was with a foot doctor. Wayne Register and I were again working together. Pam McLaney allowed us to tape her bunion surgery. There was more blood during this procedure than we had anticipated, and again, we both got sick. The surgery itself went extremely well. Two weeks after we aired the "foot surgery" story, mysteriously, the doctor left town. I was told that he had been involved in some kind of deal which got him into trouble.

...

Randall Franks, a talented Bluegrass singer and TV star, began making yearly visits to our "Morning Show" whenever he was passing through our area. Everyone at WTVY enjoyed Randall and his music. He was featured in *In the Heat of the Night* with Carroll O'Conner and Harold Rollins. An area native, David Hart, originally from Marianna, Florida, was also in the hit series.

...

Dr. Gaylon McCollough, a plastic surgeon, who grew up in Enterprise, Al, wrote a book about the newest cosmetic surgery techniques, *On the Shoulders of Giants*. I had the privilege of interviewing him at Gayfer's Department store in Wiregrass Commons Mall. The handsome doctor was swamped for autographed copies of his book.

...

Seamstress Bettie Glover became a regular on the "Morning Show" to demonstrate various sewing skills, as well as answer questions from viewer call - ins. These phone calls were a good way of getting our viewers involved. We also used the phone with various doctors and other professionals as well. Houston County Farm Agent, Reafield Vester, answered questions about lawn care and ornamentals each month. Patsy White, Home Economist with the Extension Service, gave us consumer tips, and food safety information on her monthly time slot.

The American Association for University Women provided programming to answer the unique needs and interests of our women viewers.

...

Every July, "The Morning Show" hosted an art contest. Artists from under one to over eighty entered. South Trust Bank provided cash prizes to winners in each category and the Dothan - Wiregrass Art League donated ribbons for each division. Ken Johnson, who worked as WTVY's graphics designer, coordinated this contest each year.

A memorable event was that of a teen-aged black boy who had won his category with three simple penciled drawings on notebook paper of family members. He was tremendously talented, in spite of the fact that he had been confined to bed due to a debilitating illness. (We made sure he got some proper art supplies also.)

Another contest we sponsored was "So You Want a New You." Hairstylists , make-up consultants, area department stores and a weight loss center worked together to co-sponsor the contest. Potential contestants sent us "before" pictures and explained why they wanted a "New You". A team of independent judges selected three contestants from the many letters we received.

Two of the three winners met their weight loss goal and succeeded in having a complete makeover. The third contestant who was the largest of the three, only made two appearances on the way to her goal. Her husband decided he liked her better the size she was. Perhaps he was getting a little jealous of her, because, as she began slimming down, she was getting a lot of compliments, especially, from their men friends.

...

Charles Woods had been separated from his brother when the two of them had to be placed in foster homes due to the poor health of their mother. For years, Mr. Woods had looked without success for his long lost brother. Then, one day, he got a phone call from Mr. Woods' brother's wife, Mary Morris. She had called the institution where Jack had been sent in order to try to get a copy of his birth certificate. Attached to Jack's record was the information about Mr. Woods' search for him.

The reunion was very touching, and finding out that Jack needed a job, Mr. Woods put him to work as a cameraman. Getting to know Jack Morris was a rewarding experience for everyone. He had evidently lived a very sad and lonely life. This humble man had never been exposed to some of the material things that all of us take for granted. Because Mr. Woods had been much younger than Jack, he had been adopted by P. A. Woods from Headland. Jack,by contrast, was kept at a state institution, and eventually, indentured to a farmer. The farmer mistreated Jack, and when he got older, Jack had run away. With no education and very little practical skills, he had survived by working odd jobs.

Jack was like a little boy discovering a whole new world. Even though he was nearing seventy, he was filled with wonder at every new thing he experienced. The cameras were far too complicated for Jack to handle so we had to have a backup camera operator to run camera.

When we were doing an Easter demonstration on decorating eggs, Jack just wandered away from his post to where we were illustrating the egg art.

"Miss Ann," he said. "Them eggs are the prettiest things I've ever seen. Can I hold one?"

What could I say?

Often, Jack would forget and walk right out in front of the camera. One day as Gary was in the middle of his news, Jack walked between Gary and the camera.

Jack never realized that he was doing anything wrong. Instead, he called out to Gary, "Hey, Gary, How're you doing this morning? Can I get you a cup of coffee?"

Everyone loved Jack. He was the gentlest, sweetest little man. When he was diagnosed with terminal cancer, he was really afraid to die. I visited him in the hospital and had the privilege of leading him to Christ. The last thing that he said to me with a big smile on his face was,

"Thank you, Miss Ann, now I'm not afraid to die. God is with me!" Jack died shortly afterwards.

...

Every Year before the annual Bonifay Rodeo, members of the Kiwanis Club always brought rodeo riders or clowns out to do our program. One year they chose to bring a championship horse. As we were carrying the horse into the studio, he suddenly stumbled and fell on the slippery studio floor. His trainer had failed to cover his hoofs with the proper non-slip covers. He fell, strangely enough, between the camera and Gary Bruce, who was just about to do the weather. Gary had to go on while the poor horse moaned and groaned as he tried to get up. Thinking quickly, our cameraman shot Gary up high so no one could see the horse.

Right after the weather, the trainer put a piece of carpet under the horse and was able to drag him gently out of the studio. (Another example of Gary's ability to be the unshakable professional.)

···

I had read the book *Run Baby Run* years before I met the man that the book had been written about. Nicky Cruz had been a drug addict and gang leader in New York City when a Pentecostal preacher named David Wilkerson had come to town. Nicky had tried in every way to make fun of this country preacher. Instead, Nicky Cruz had surrendered to the power of love. His life was dramatically changed when he gave his life to Jesus Christ. When I interviewed him, he was traveling across the country sharing with teenagers that you don't have to go along with the crowd. "One person," he said, "willing to stand up for right can make a difference!"

Nicky Cruz also discussed the importance of fathers being the heroes in their homes. "If a father takes his rightful place in the home," Nicky insisted, "not only will his wife and family feel loved and secure, but it will keep the children out of trouble. I am my four daughters' number one hero. They see how I love their mother, so they aren't willing to settle for anything less."

(What a tremendous change in a man who had once been a vicious gang leader.)

···

Charlie Gilmore, the host of a classic country show on WTVY - FM, brought the legendary Jerry Reed by for a visit one morning. Between the two of them, they pretty much took over the show. Some people called to complain, however, because they both put their big boots on the top of my coffee table. Jerry Reed was a natural comedian and very nice to all of us. He put on a dynamite show later that evening at the Houston County Farm Center.

...

Wayne Rader invited us down to do a special at Panama City Beach, Florida, with his whole family at the Ocean Opry. One thing for sure, you couldn't be a member of the Rader family unless you could sing, act, play a musical instrument or otherwise entertain. From the youngest grandchild to the grandparents, all were performers. The Ocean Opry provides good, clean family fun. We enjoyed every minute of our visit.

...

Spending a week-end at Seaside, Florida, was something I could get used to. We were invited down to so an hour special on this almost magical little village. The owner, Robert Davis, confided in me that his grandfather had purchased the tract of land that had later become Seaside for only a few hundred dollars years before. No one would have ever believed it could have become the nostalgic resort that it has become today.

We toured the shops, homes, and art exhibits and sampled the wonderful food in the various eating places.

Phillip Bump and his wife Debbie were able to join me and my husband Jerome. Phillip did a great job of helping me put the special together. The response to that show was immediate and very gratifying.

...

My sons were fascinated that I was going to get to meet Mike Warneke, a comedian who claimed that he had once been a witch. The interview with Mr. Warneke was held at the Dothan Civic Center right before his performance. I certainly didn't like the stories he told about his years in witchcraft, but all of us enjoyed his hilarious comedy. The entertainer explained to a packed house that night that God had a great sense of humor.

"When he wants you," Mike grinned, "he'll get you! He sent the weirdest roommates to me in boot camp. They were all Christians. I was a witch! Guess who won? They did! God finally got a hold of me, and I've never been the same since!"

...

It has been a tradition at Christmas, that one of our WTVY employees - usually Wayne Register - would dress up like Santa Claus and appear on our "Morning Show." This visit by our "Santa" was always a fun thing to do until I met a man who said he was the real Santa Claus. He even looked the part in every way. Although this man had a regular job, he kept his snowy white hair and matching beard trimmed just like Santa would, and he always wore a red tie!

We begged him to come back for a visit around Christmas time. He reluctantly agreed, protesting strongly, that he really had too much work to do around the Holiday Season to come back to WTVY. (There was a definite twinkle in his eye when he said this.)

On the appointed date for his appearance on our program, he walked in completely outfitted in the most authentic Santa outfit I had ever seen. He not only looked just like Santa Claus, he talked like I always thought Santa would talk. Gary just lifted his eyebrows. (Had Santa really come to town?) We got calls for days about this Santa. He left us a card which simply read, "Santa Clause, North Pole - Merry Christmas!"

...

Gary, Teresa and I had the privilege of interviewing "Miss Black America." She was a lovely young woman who looked more like a teenager than an adult woman. We were all shocked to learn that in the ensuing months after her visit with us, she had been the person who had accused Boxer Mike Tyson of rape. Mike was subsequently sentenced to prison as a result of this crime.

Chapter Eleven
WTVY moves to downtown Dothan

Charles Woods had purchased the old Houston Hotel in downtown Dothan. For many years, the building had housed Troy State University. I knew Mr. Woods wanted to move WTVY, but I never thought that he would move us downtown.

It took a long time to do all the renovations necessary for us to be able to relocate. Architect Joe Donofro worked with each of us at WTVY to determine what our specific needs would be for the new building. Becky Copeland and Judy Calhoun had the responsibility of decorating the new station. They did a wonderful job.

One Saturday all of WTVY 's employees met at the old building to begin the long move. We were so impressed at the complete transformation of the downtown location. Everything had been perfectly designed to work like clockwork. We were ready to go on the air the following Monday morning.

In a few weeks after our move, Dothan's dignitaries and WTVY employees joined in a very special dedication service which was aired around 10:00 in the morning. I had the privilege of being the mistress of ceremonies for the big event. Mr. Woods' daughter Scarlett was the "little star" of the day.

Former WTVY "on air" personalities joined us for live interviews. Betty Gault and John Gause enjoyed reflecting on their years on camera at WTVY. Country Western star Mark Collie dropped by for a visit. (I also caught up with him again when he was a special guest of the National Peanut Festival. His song, "Even the Man is the Moon is Crying," was already number one on the country charts.)

Getting used to a new set, a new building and a completely different format was interesting to say the least. Our "Morning Show" had been airing from 8:00 - 9:00 a.m. for years, and our ratings were very good at that time slot. My new challenge was "driving from Webb to Dothan now!" For 18 ½ years we lived in Dothan; hence, I had made the trip to Webb every morning. When we bought Red Holland 's house in Webb, I was two minutes from work for six and a half months. Then, WTVY moved to Dothan. I had to reverse myself and drive from Webb to Dothan. (Life is interesting!)

It was not long after we moved to our new studio, that Mr. Woods sold WTVY-TV to the Chemical Bank of New York. Don Tomlin and Jack Quick came to oversee WTVY until they could find a new owner for our station. This was an especially difficult time for us. When the new bosses came in, many of our co-workers were given termination notices. It was sad to see our friends have to pack up their desks and leave. (This always happens today in corporate America, I'm told.)

Once the major changes were accomplished, we found out that our new management really had our best interests at heart. Mr. Tomlin was primarily the negotiator who worked to upgrade our station in preparation for potential buyers. Jack Quick became the "hands on" man that we usually communicated with.

Innovative Jack, came up with the idea of enlarging our show to include a regular Panama City feature. Linda Scott, who had moved to Dothan from that area, was sent back to Panama City to do this part of our program in addition to covering news stories. The "Morning Show" was expanded to an hour and a half and aired from 8:00-9:30 a.m. It was fun to talk with Linda each day via our microwave hook-up.

Almost immediately, Gary Bruce, Teresa Thomas and I had set up a Friday breakfast club. Linda Scott also featured breakfast in Panama City on these days. Linda reported on the news from Panama City and the surrounding towns while we primarily did features on the Wiregrass area.

...

Dr. Ken Dunn, a doctor of Natureopathy began a monthly visit on the "Morning Show" to talk about various herbal remedies. It became one of our most popular features. As individuals are exploring healthier lifestyles, alternative health care is becoming a great avenue for many of these individuals. Ken was so pleased with the response that he got that he immediately became one of our best advertisers. He also wrote a letter to Station Manager Don Tomlin to compliment the "Morning Show 's effectiveness.

Trying to capitalize on a successful venture, Ken and I began doing commercials together. We might be selling weight loss products one week and herbal tonics the next. Whatever the case, I became a strong supporter of many products which seemed to help me personally.

Our funniest commercial to date has been one we shot at Landmark Park. Ken and I were promoting a complete vitamin and mineral health tonic called "Maximum Advantage". At the beginning of the commercial, we discussed feeling "dragged out". Next, we both drank some of the product. The following scene showed us pulling the lever to an old cane mill as we ran faster and faster around the building. We eventually had to walk around the cane mill about twenty-five times to shoot enough footage for Brenda Steffin and Brad Matherne in our creative services department to be able to speed up the video in order to create the desired effect. The commercial really was effective even if we did get laughed at about how funny we looked with our short little fat legs running around the cane mill.

...

Every Friday, Gary and I hosted a "Pet of the Week" segment sponsored by the Wiregrass Humane Society. It has been interesting to see how many dogs, cats, kittens and puppies have been adopted through someone seeing a pet on TV. Twice, our "Morning Show" guests have even adopted the pet of the week. One of our "Miss Alabama" queens adopted a charcoal gray kitten. Another time, a visiting romance novelist adopted the "dog of her dreams" to replace a deceased family pet. (This dog even attended her autograph party that same afternoon. He behaved as if he had always belonged to her.)

One month, I featured a "Pet of the Week" reunion. Many of our viewers who had adopted pets from our show brought the pet back to tell about the joy they had found with this particular animal. One man brought a tiny little furry dog who must have thought he was a "world champion prize fighter!" He took on every dog there - male or female. The huge dogs just stared at him or growled. One big dog even cowered down at the little dog's attack. At one point during the show, the master had to isolate his little dog from the rest of the pets in order to keep peace.

The owner explained, "He never gives us any trouble at home. I just don't think he likes dogs!"

...

One of my own dogs, Jake, a mixed Lab-Chow, had been missing for a number of months when Teresa Thomas and I were sent to Panama City to do a remote from the Hombre Golf course. On the way down, as we were driving through Alford, Florida, I looked up just in time to see my dog Jake running toward Dothan on the other side of the big four lane highway. I'm sure Teresa thought I had lost my mind when I told her to go back because of this dog. By the time we found a place to turn around, the big black dog was taking off into the woods. All at once, I began to have second thoughts about this dog really being my Jake. Overcoming my doubts, I called to him, and he froze in his tracks. He came bounding back down the hill and jumped right into my arms. It was like a *Lassie Come Home* movie. I was in tears, it was raining, and Jake was doing his best to wash my entire face with his tongue.

The most astounding thing was that I not only found my dog, but I had a client, CBS Trading Co. in Alford, who kept Jake for me until my husband could come down and pick him up. Teresa and I were then able to continue our trip to Panama City without much delay.

I have told all about the "Jake" story in a children's book I have written called, *Jake, the Prodigal Dog.* God really does care about everything which concerns His children. I had prayed that I would be able to find Jake if he were still alive. The chances of Jake being on the same highway just as we were passing by were phenomenal. We don't know how Jake got to Florida, but he has never left home again.

While at the Hombre in Panama City Beach, I had the opportunity to interview Dave Thomas, the founder of Wendy's hamburgers. He was such a successful businessman who gave credit to God completely for his accomplishments. (He really does have a daughter named Wendy.)

"Spanky" McFarland was another guest celebrity I had the privilege of interviewing at the golf club. (He was the adorable, chubby-cheeked child star of the *Our Gang* movie series.) Mr. McFarland told me wonderful stories about how he got the role, the way scenes were set up for the movies, and how "Spot", the dog, had to have the ring repainted around his eye each day.

Another bit of information that he related had to do with a hoax being pulled by an "Alfalfa" impersonator. It seems that quite by accident, "Spanky" McFarland had caught a TV interview with this man who was pretending to be "Alfalfa"(the skinny , freckled faced boy whose hair always parted in the middle and spiked at the top.) The real "Alfalfa" had been dead for years (supposedly, from a drug overdose). Mr. McFarland then got in touch with the TV station and exposed the impersonator.

"What happened to the man who was pretending to be Alfalfa?", I asked.

"I haven't the slightest idea," he answered. "I just did what I needed to do."

(Only a few months after my interview, Mr. McFarland died, himself, from heart failure.)

I caught up with Bobby Bowden, the football coach of the Championship F.S.U. Seminoles just as he was exiting the golf course. For some reason, he agreed to do an interview with me. (I was the only station who got the chance.) I was so impressed with Coach Bowden's obvious love for his wife and his sons. He emphasized home and family, as well as, football goals.

Right after he left, his son Terry was completing his golf game when I walked on the green to talk to him.

"I just completed an interview with your father, Coach Bowden", I said. "I'm also an big Auburn fan, can I get a few quick comments from you also?"

He nodded and I started. The camera was already rolling. Coach Terry Bowden also expressed great pride in his father not only as a gifted football coach, but as a devoted father.

"He taught us much more about the game of life than he ever did about the game of football." Coach Terry Bowden declared.

Thereupon, he was off to an awaiting car which took him to an airplane to fly back to Auburn University. I was so pleased over "snagging" both interviews.

(I don't think one of the young sports anchors at a Panama City station likes me very much. He didn't get an interview with either coach.)

Soap star and heart-throb Jack Wagner was also trying his hand at the charity golf tournament. I caught up with him just as he was beginning his game the next morning. I have learned to be bold, and I always tell Phil to keep the camera running.

So far, no one has told me "No!" to a request for an interview except two people. One was Sammy Kershaw, a country western singer and performer at the National Peanut Festival. He was extremely arrogant to everyone, including Peanut Festival executives who were paying his fees, and also, to all autograph seekers. His road manager was trying to get him to allow us to interview him, but he flatly refused.

The only other interview I failed to get was with Stella Parton, Dolly Parton's sister. I was planning to do an interview with her one night at a big show at the Dothan Civic Center between the two performances. It seems that she declined because she needed to have her hair washed and styled before the second show. I did catch up with the famed "Grandpa Jones" later that night. He was a great comedic actor. (I finally did get an interview with Stella Parton when we met her in Clayton, Alabama with old friend Randy Franks. They were starring in a movie together about the future of our planet. It was to be shot entirely in and around Clayton, Al. by Galaxy entertainment.)

...

Barbara Bush came through Dothan to campaign for her husband George during his bid for the presidency of the United States. I had wanted very much to get an interview with her; therefore, I joined the media representatives at a local motel. The room was crowded with television and newspaper journalist from three states at least. A CBS correspondent was also there doing a day by day report on

Mrs. Bush's campaign stops. I knew my chances were slim to get a private, personal interview with her, but I prayed that I might be able to somehow pull it off. Just about the time I had about given up hope, I looked up to spot my friend Anita Folmar, wife of Montgomery mayor Emory Folmar, standing right beside Barbara Bush. She had also just recognized me in the crowd. Anita began motioning for me to join her. In expectation, I pushed through the crowd with my cameraman, Phillip Bump, right behind me.

Anita said when I managed to get to her, "Barbara, this is my friend Ann Varnum. She needs to do an interview with you."

That was all it took. Security guards ushered us off to a private room, and I got my interview with the charming Mrs. Bush who was soon to become the first lady of our country. I'll never forget how personable she was, and how kind she was to everyone. The Tammy Wynette song "Stand By Your Man" kept playing in my ears after our interview. I was thoroughly convinced that this devoted wife and mother was the bedrock of George Bush's life.

...

When the movie about the life of Nora Lam was scheduled to be presented at the Dothan Civic Center, I was necessarily swept up in all the preparations for the big event.

Special celebrity guests from the Tri-States were scheduled to be in Dothan for the viewing of the movie about the life of this Chinese woman who had managed to survive communist oppression. Nora had been converted to Christianity as a young university student. At one point, she was placed in front of a firing squad and shot. For some mysterious reason, (God's providential care, she says) not one bullet touched her. The soldiers who manned the firing squad were so terrified when she was still standing, that they all began yelling in fear and ran away. After surviving many other such terrible circumstances in her life, Nora had finally been able to come to America.

I had the opportunity to interview Nora Lam in one of the Dothan Civic Center's beautiful reception rooms before the movie of her life was shown. Mrs. Lam was one of the most energetic, lovable and dynamic women I had ever met. Even though she would now be considered a senior citizen, there was nothing "old" about Nora Lam. She still had the sparkle and enthusiasm of a young woman.

"Jesus made it all possible for me," she said in an animated voice. "Nora did nothing, Jesus did it all! I wanted to tell my story so that others in my country can know the truth. Now, through this film it will be told!"

Following my conversation with Nora Lam, I also interviewed some of the other stars in the movie. David Soul's wife, Julie, played the role of Nora, while France Nuyen starred as Nora's mother.

The film was breathtaking, the acting excellent, and the story was tremendously moving. The next day after the film had been shown, Nora invited me to go to China with her. (Doors had been opened for her to show the *Nora Lam Story* in her homeland of China.) How I wish that I could have gone with her, but it was just impossible at the time. A number of my friends did go with Nora, and one of then was a former WTVY on-air personality, Laurie Lynn Benson Morris.

...

The day that Adrien Arpel walked into our new studio in downtown Dothan, I knew that I had come face to face with a grand lady. "Class" was written all over her. She was in town to do a seminar at Gayfer's on "doing the best for yourself that you can do."

Her first comments to me were, "Ann, I think your building is prettier than Ophrah's" Following this remark, she was very complimentary on my choice of colors that I was wearing.

When it was time to go on the show, she already seemed like an old friend. With absolute ease, she went right through her make-over secrets, which were very insightful and practical.

She gave tips on concealing facial blemishes, dressing according to one's body build and size, and covering up your faults and maximizing your assets. When we flashed the number on the screen for viewers to call for reservations to her seminar, we got as many calls from Panama City as Dothan. We were all delighted at the instant response.

That afternoon, Teresa Thomas and I attended her seminar. We learned so many great ideas about how to coordinate your wardrobe (while saving on your budget). Ms Arpel also encouraged women of all sizes to, "Let your true beauty show through no matter what you weigh. Be the best that you can be," she remarked with authority.

...

I interviewed author and inspirational speaker, Dr. Peter Marshall, during the National Peanut Festival one year. He was in Dothan to speak at a conference at the First

Presbyterian Church. His two books, *The Light and the Glory* and its sequel, *From Sea to Shining Sea*, which he co-authored with David Manuel, described in accurate detail the true spiritual, as well as the historical purpose of our country. Once you start reading either one of the books, you simply can't put them down.

Dr. Marshall's father, Peter Marshall, Sr., had served as the chaplain for the U. S. Senate before his untimely death with a heart attack. Peter Marshall's mother, Catherine Marshall, was also a world famous Christian author. Her book *Christy*, about the life of her mother, had later been made into a TV series.

Talking with Dr. Marshall was like a breath of fresh air. He was so knowledgeable, and yet, so basic in his beliefs. My cameraman kept winding me up before I finally called for a break. I confess. I am a big fan of Dr. Peter Marshall.

...

It has always been my desire to have high quality programs. No matter who I interview or where I travel, I am always looking for new and different ideas. Some of my favorite interviews have been with someone who might be your next door neighbor or with a "little known" artist who is later discovered. I truly enjoy talking with people from all walks of life.

The new "Morning Show" format seemed to be working really well with the four of us, Gary, Teresa, Linda and I interacting. At that time our program was still the longest running talk show in Alabama with the same hostess - me. One morning, Jack Quick invited the entire staff of WTVY to walk on our show to congratulate me on my 20th anniversary. The anniversary cake they presented to me almost caught fire with all those candles on it. This incident added the needed touch of humor to the event to keep me from getting too emotional.

...

Garth Brooks was probably one of the biggest stars the Peanut Festival had ever signed a contract with. The night of his performance, it was good that my cameraman and I got backstage early because the crowd was enormous. No mater what, it was well worth the wait. What a pleasant young man this superstar is. He was so polite with his "Ma'ams" when he addressed me. He even looked into the camera to personally give a message to my nephew, Jack Lavallet, who had been confined to a wheelchair after his diving accident. (Jack was thrilled that someone he had admired so much would take the time to say, "Hang in there, Jack, you're going to do okay.", on television, directly to him.)

Not only did we have a successful interview, but we stayed for his outstanding show. To tell the truth, we had no choice. The crowd was so packed that we couldn't have left if we had chosen to do so. At the end of the second show, I was told that Garth Brooks had stayed and signed autographs until 2:00 a.m. (No wonder he has made it to the top of his profession. He cares for his fans!)

Chapter Twelve
Changes, changes, changes.....

Jack Quick has truly become a great friend to me. He always considered my opinion before making any changes which would affect me or my position. By reason of the fact that I was head of Public Affairs (in addition to hosting "The Morning Show"), he often asked me to take care of a complaint or respond to a question from a viewer. One thing that Jack Quick and Don Tomlin did - they responded to all letters that we received - good or bad.

One night we had a big reception in Panama City. Many dignitaries from all over the area were invited to attend. It was truly a big gala event, but most of us were not feeling very festive. We had just been notified that Benedek Broadcasting had just purchased WTVY. That meant more changes and the possibility of losing even more co-workers.

...

The first night I met our new owners, I was running late to the dinner at the Highland Oaks Golf Club which was held in their honor. My ladies' Bible Class had it's annual Christmas covered-dish dinner at my home that night. Therefore, not only did I have to get someone to teach for me, but I had to make sure that everything was set up properly for my guests. I was so torn between the two responsibilities that I didn't realize how long it would take for me to make it to Highland Oaks. When I walked in late after everyone was seated, there was only one chair left - right beside the new owner, Richard Benedek. Seeing me come in, this nice gentleman jumped up, took my coat and made me feel right at home. Our conversation that night ran the gamut from a discussion about my former boss Charles Woods, to future plans for WTVY.

•••

True, some more of our coworkers were dismissed when Benedek took over, but more of us stayed than we had thought possible. I gave Jack Quick and Don Tomlin a little memento when they left, plus a note of thanks. Jack got a "guardian angel" with folded wings, while I gave Don Tomlin a "guardian angel" with wings ready for flight. I told Jack he provided the roots for Don. On the other hand, Don was always "taking off" with one of his exciting visions. They made a great team, and I knew we would miss them. All in all, they had treated us wonderfully well.

•••

More changes were in store. The Panama City segment was continued for awhile but Christine Alombro did the interviews. Linda Scott was no longer with us.

Every time we made changes of any kind, we got calls - usually to complain. And, answering complaints was part of my job, I had to try to handle these calls and smooth over any problems.

It was not long before the new WTVY management made still another change. They canceled the "Morning Show", took Gary Bruce and Teresa Thomas off the program and changed the show to "Morning Talk". Linda Scott was invited back to co-host the show with me from Panama City. Our show time slot was also moved to 9:00 a.m. There again, the phones rang as viewers complained about the changes.

Linda Scott and I did everything we knew to do to make the show work. The features from Panama City included: Car Talk, Law Talk and a regular Exercise Talk. Linda and I visited together every morning via our microwave equipment. A few times, we experienced technical problems and couldn't pick up the Panama City interviews. That left me with the responsibility of filling the time for the entire hour.

The sales department came up with the idea of having sponsors for some of our "Morning Talk" segments. Ken Dunn agreed to do a sponsorship in order to share the news on the latest herbal products. Nick Slaughter brought sewing tips from Derrell's Sewing Center. Nancy Prim, a very talented fashion coordinator represented Gayfer's with news from the fashion world. The Dothan Area Botanical Gardens spotlighted Russell Tedder with tips on gardening. We still had time to do other interviews during our individual time slots. Every effort was made to keep our program interesting. We even tried shooting "on the shoulder" with our camera as we walked through some scenes on location. Because of all our hard work, Linda and I thought the program was moving along rather well when we were informed that there was still another change to be made.

"Morning Talk" was canceled and I was given the new "Morning Show" to host by myself. This time I only had thirty minutes for the program which aired from 9:00-9:30 a.m. Callers complained about the show being shortened.

With my new format, I tried to come up with even better programming ideas. Mark Aldridge brought Mary Ellen Withrow, the Treasurer of the United States, to visit with me one morning. Ms. Withrow was in our area to promote the purchasing of U. S. Savings Bonds. She kindly re-signed some of our dollar bills. Ms. Withrow's style and presence was very impressive. I told her that she had a standing invitation to come back any time she was in our area.

Always one of our best features on our talk show has been our cooking segments. K. W. Keene from WOOF radio, City Manager Jerry Gwaltney, City Commissioner Chester Sowell (who was soon elected Mayor), City Commissioner Don Clements, Australian native Robert Cazelet, WTVY's Mitch English, Larry Talton from Winn Dixie's Marketplace, Larry Dealey from Grate Things and many others joined the ranks as our celebrity chefs. The amount of recipe requests was still a good indication of how many viewers we had.

To surprise me, one spring morning, my former co-host Don Day from WLWI dropped by for a visit. He simply ran on the set and gave me a big hug and kiss. I love spontaneous programming!

To continue an expanded news format, Michile Smith Lam and Phil Robertson started "WTVY This Morning" which aired from 6:00-7:00 a.m. Red Holland was still seen on WTVY from 5:00-6:00 a.m. and "CBS This Morning" was shown from 7:00-9:00 a.m. (I had always wanted my original time slot back, but it seemed impossible at the time.)

As WTVY's Public Affairs Director, I am constantly called upon to speak on behalf of WTVY. On one trip to Ozark, Alabama, our new station manager, Tom Wall, accompanied me. I was scheduled to speak to the Ozark Kiwanis Club at the invitation of my friend, Wyatt Belcher. While traveling over, I told Tom that he was a very brave man. When he looked at me a little puzzled, I replied, "I'm driving, and you don't seem nervous at all."

After returning to Dothan, when we drove back into WTVY 's parking lot, many of our production crew were standing outside the building. As Tom got out of the car, they all began to laugh and say, "You survived! You made it back in one piece."

Tom spoke up on my behalf.

"Actually," he said, "Ann is a very good driver. We had no problems at all."

(Little did he know ... but that's another story.)

...

The outstanding pianist Jim Brickman made an appearance on our new "Morning Show." I arranged for him to have the entire program. Not only does he write and play beautiful music, but he has a tremendous gift for composing musical commercials. Much of the theme music and catchy phrases behind some of the best television commercials of today were all written by Jim Brickman.

One of the fun parts of that particular program came when Jim went over to our studio piano to play some of his compositions. "Don't treat your puppy like a dog, dog, dog ...feed him Purina Puppy Chow!" Then, he played the alluring background music for a sleek new Revlon lipstick commercial. What a talented guy he is! He told me that his grandmother had been the one to inspire and encourage him to play the piano. The late Jim Henson, creator of the Muppets, had also taken Jim Brickman "under his wing" when Jim was still a teenager. He said that he got his first job with the famed Muppet creator.

...

Steve Walker, Chaplain of the Bullock County Prison, invited me to do a program on the rehabilitation services offered to inmates at this particular institution.

It may seem funny, but I was a little nervous about having to go into a prison. My thoughts were racing as to how I would be able to handle the interviews. Chaplain Walker put my mind at ease.

"Ann, I have secured permission from our warden and from the prisoners who have volunteered to be interviewed. Ask whatever you want to ask." Steve assured me.

Steve Walker's dream was to offer educational and spiritual guidance to the toughest inmates, as well as to those with the usual drug and alcohol problems. His system appeared to be very effective. (In fact, today, Governor Fob James has recognized it as the state's prototype for the rehabilitation of prisoners.)

My first interview was with a very handsome, clean-cut young man named David. His father was a minister but David had, at an early age, chosen to get involved with the wrong crowd. During one of his wild drinking sprees, he had killed someone. Already, he had been in prison twelve years with very little chance of parole. David told me that he was no longer the same person who had committed that crime. "I gave my life to Christ," he explained, "and, no matter what happens to me in this life, I have peace. God has forgiven me for all my sins including the murder I committed."

At that, I could hardly hold back the tears.

Next, I talked to a genial looking man with gray hair. As he told me his story, I admit, I was not prepared for what he said.

"I am serving this prison term because I committed incest with my daughter. I'm so ashamed of what I did. At the time that I wronged my child, I just seemed powerless to stop. Thanks to Chaplain Walker, I have made things right with God. I only pray that my wife and daughter can some day find it in their hearts to forgive me!" he tearfully closed.

Whereas the first two men gave no clue by their appearance as to the type of crime that they had committed, this was not the case of the third inmate I interviewed. The man named Terry had steel blue eyes and sat with his head slightly drooped as he talked.

"I am a child molester", he began, "and if they don't keep me locked up in here, I'll do it again. I can't help myself. I don't care if it's boys or girls. I just have a craving I can't satisfy."

In the ensuing moments, it appeared that he had a change in attitude while he continued to stare at me with those cold, blue eyes.

"You want to know how I get them to go with me?" he said in a boastful manner. (I didn't want to know.)

"Never mind," I brusquely cut him off. He tried to tell me the number of children he had molested, and I felt hot water coming up in my throat. It was as if he were beginning to gloat about his deeds. I was feeling sick.

His last statement was, "I just ride around until I see some children out playing. It's like 'feeding the pig'. The more you see them, the more you want to do it …. I can't help what I do."

Abruptly, I ended the interview. I didn't want to lose my lunch in front of the camera. (It was obvious there had been no help yet for this man.)

"Steve, I think I have all the interviews I need." I said to Chaplain Walker.

A nice looking young black man came over then and offered to help us carry our equipment back to the main exit. He seemed so pleasant and nice I couldn't resist whispering to Chaplain Walker, "What's he in for?"

"Three counts of rape." Steve whispered back. (A tough investigative reporter I am not.)

•••

Pat Robertson was campaigning for the Presidency of the United States. Two of his ardent supporters, Richard Arthur and Dan Smith, invited me and Phil Bump to fly with them to Atlanta to do an interview with Mr. Robertson. I thought it would be a lot of fun so we said "Yes!"

Little did I know what was awaiting me that morning. I wore my very best hunter green wool suit with a white silk blouse. I wanted to be appropriately dressed for the occasion. We left so early that Saturday morning, that I had only taken time to drink a few swallows of a low calorie soft drink before boarding the small airplane. As we buckled our seat belts, we noticed that the sky was getting very dark and the wind was beginning to pick up.

By the time we left Dothan, the turbulence was so bad that I began to feel very, very sick. Finally, I could not help myself. I began to throw up violently - all over my white silk blouse, the suit, the floor - everywhere! Richard Arthur was in the back with me, and he did everything he could to help. Nothing seemed to relieve my nausea. I kept apologizing, but I kept right on throwing up.

After awhile, Phil Bump, who was in the front seat, started throwing up too. It was so embarrassing. Both of us had flown many times before and had never been sick on other flights. Neither Richard nor Dan got sick. They simply tried their best to look after us.

When at last we arrived at the Atlanta airport, I ran into the ladies restroom and whipped off my blouse. I washed it thoroughly in the sink using the soap from the liquid dispenser. After spotting my suit, I fully intended to air-dry my sopping wet blouse. You guessed it! There was no hot air dryer! For the first time in my life I wanted, and needed, a hot air dryer, and there was only paper towel. I couldn't believe it! I had no choice but to pat my blouse dry as best I could with paper towel and put my very wet blouse back on. There was no way I could wear my suit without a blouse because of the way it was cut.

Just as I got through in the bathroom, it was beginning to turn really cold. My wet blouse didn't help matters either. Because of our appointment, we had to rush in order to get to the hotel where the interview was to be done.

It was well worth all the trouble I had endured when I met Pat Robertson. The ten minutes I spent talking to him seemed like seconds because our conversation went so smoothly. Most people do not realize how very scholarly and intelligent Mr. Robertson really is. He is a graduate of Harvard Law School with a degree in law, business and a minor in journalism.

After our visit with Mr. Robertson ended, Phil and I honestly considered renting a car to take us back to Dothan. As an alternative, we took some air sick pills and flew back sitting very, very still. Thank goodness, we didn't get sick on the way home.

(By the time I got back to WTVY on Monday morning, Jerry Vann's version of the story had me throwing up on Pat Robertson. Shame on you, Jerry.)

...

Dr. Barry Burkhalt, a clinical psychiatrist, granted me permission to come to Opelika to tape a special with him on his work with sex offenders. Ever since my experience at Bullock County Prison, I had wanted to know more about what happened to the inmates who were guilty of these kinds of crimes when they were released from prison.

When I asked Dr. Burkhalt why he did what he did, he responded, "For years I have been trying to rescue victims of sex crimes from the swelling tide of their circumstances. At length I began to want to find out more about who was throwing them in."

Dr. Burkhalt, to my knowledge, is the only person in Alabama who oversees a "Support Group" for sex offenders. It is set up very much like Alcoholics Anonymous. Men are required by their parole officers to regularly attend these weekly meetings. The group also acts as a monitoring system for each other. "No one wants to fail," Dr. Burkhalt said. "They try to keep each other from repeating the same patterns that got them in trouble in the first place." he added.

When I asked about the expression, "feeding the pig", which Terry, the child molester, had used in the interview I had done at the Bullock County Prison, Dr. Burkhalt nodded.

"Yes, that is a term sex offenders use routinely." he further detailed. "It means doing something that will continually increase the desire to act out one's fantasies, very much like continuing to stuff a pig. My men know when someone in the group is doing this, and they try to stop him before it's too late."

Dr. Burkhalt said that he didn't believe there was ever a cure for this deviate behavior. "The support group has worked so well that I have had only one client who had to be sent back to prison for a sex offense in the six or so years since the group has been formed". he declared with authority.

...

Len and Debbie Mattox are the owners of the delightful Sasquatch Zoo between Crestview and DeFuniak Springs, Florida. Once, a flood nearly washed their entire operation away, causing them to move to a higher location. By the time the "Morning Show" visited their zoo, everything was set up in perfect order. We couldn't believe the wide variety of animals housed in their natural habitats.

My favorite animals were the monkeys. When we were there, a mother monkey had just given birth to a tiny little baby. The proud father was pounding his chest and showing his teeth to us. Often, he would go over and put his arm around the female and even pat the baby. I thought it was so very sweet.

Len Mattox informed us that just as soon as the baby began to be weaned, the father would totally change in behavior.

"If we don't take the baby out soon enough, the older male will try to kill it," Len explained. "I guess it's something about the male dominance thing."

Another little monkey, "Baby Sarah" had been abandoned by her mother, and Debbie was raising her at home like a child. Sarah wore diapers and drank from a bottle. My grandchildren, Brandi and Amber, wanted to take the baby monkey home. It was evident that all the children visiting the zoo that day loved Baby Sarah.

Every visitor to the zoo was also fascinated by the teenage lion Debbie had raised. This brave lady could go into the lion's shelter at any time and wrestle with her pet. It seemed like he simply knew not to play too rough with Debbie.

As a special favor to the army, the Mattoxes were called upon to keep two camels for an extended period of time. These desert creatures had been presented to the military by dignitaries from one of the Middle Eastern countries. In preparation for the proper "housing" of these added guests, Len and Debbie had to do some research to create just the right living facilities for these unusual beasts. They accomplished it in a short period of time, much to their credit.

Through the years, Len and Debbie continue to make appearances on our program. Not only does Debbie have a decided closeness with certain animals, but Len, himself, acts as a "mother" figure to some of the huge exotic birds who bond to him. They give Len kisses and squawk if anyone tries to touch Len.

...

Michile Lam and Phil Robertson left "WTVY This Morning" during the height of their show's success to pursue opportunities in other cities. Michile's husband had to do an internship at the University Hospital in Birmingham, and Phil got a chance to go to a station in a larger market. All of us hated to see the two of them leave because they were very good at what they did.

Mary Hughes, Gary Bruce and Mitch English were then assigned to the 6:00 - 7:00 a.m. time slot. Teresa Thomas had also been moved to news.

...

Always looking for ways to bring in more viewers, WTVY started doing our "Home Town" Salutes. In each city we recognized, our news team would cover the different features of that town which made it unique. The first city we highlighted was Enterprise, Alabama. Some of the nicest people in the world live in Enterprise.

Mayor Johnny Henderson rolled out the proverbial red carpet for us. It was also fun working with old friends like Jim and Lucy Klein at the West Gate Book and Gift Shop. The Kleins chose to live in Enterprise primarily because of the friendliness of one of the local police officers. It seems that the officer had driven by just as Jim was peering into a vacant store window. The Kleins were looking for a place to put their business . Instead of treating Jim like an "intruder" or potential criminal, the kindly officer asked Jim if he might help him in any way. (Speaking of making a good impression.)

Our next city was Ozark, Alabama. I did our "Morning Show" downtown at "The Painted Place", in one of the art districts. The Dale County RSVP visited us, as well as students from the Ozark Boys and Girls Club. Many of the very talented artists of the area including Jack Deloney stopped by to do an interview with us.

The next "Home Town" salute was Marianna, Florida. Our crew got to stay in a beautiful bed n' breakfast, The Hinson House. Later our "Morning Show" was broadcast from "Interiors by Gayle" in downtown Marianna. This was a beautiful interior design studio. Each division was set up like a room in someone's home. The morning of the live broadcast, right in the middle of a cooking demonstration in their kitchen, the smoke detector went off. Not only did the owner, Gayle Howard, not know that she had a smoke detector, but she didn't know where it was! It was an interesting cooking segment with the loud smoke detector "beeping" in the background, coupled with the noise of our engineers scurrying to locate it. (The joys of live TV.)

...

CBS aired the TV mini series, *The Last Confederate Widow*. Steve, our oldest son, had a small role in Part II of the series. Even though the CBS program was pure fiction, I interviewed the genuine last confederate widow in Elba, Alabama, Mrs. Alberta Martin. She had a wonderful story to tell me. It seems that she was a young widowed single parent when she met the elderly former Confederate soldier, Mr. Martin. He was kind to her, and he had a good pension. Mrs. Martin told me that it had been a good marriage.

"In fact," she smiled, "we even had a son together. He treated me good."

...

When Tom Nebel left WTVY to manage WDJR radio, Gary Bruce was moved back to WTVY 's six and ten o'clock weather slot. Joey Parker joined Mary Hughes and Mitch English on "WTVY This Morning". They made a great team.

In a very short time, Joey and Mitch had become part of my extended family. Mitch had been a D. J. at WDJR radio, and Tom Nebel helped him get started as a weatherman on the early news at 6:00 a.m. "Uninhibited" is a mild word to describe Mitch. He is a weatherman of a completely different breed. Viewers love him!

...

As the National Peanut Festival grew larger each year, every effort was made to bring in the best country, gospel and pop groups for entertainment. John Stamos, star of *Full House* , the hit TV series, gave us a wonderful interview, but his rock music was not my style. A country favorite, Charlie Daniels, is a really tall man who is not only a super patriot, a great musician and a fun person to talk to, but he is also a very dedicated Christian who freely expresses his faith.

Tanya Tucker really shined at her shows at the National Peanut Festival. When I met with her, all she could talk about was her upcoming fishing trip to Quincey, Florida, after leaving Dothan. Tanya said next to her child, she loves fishing most.

Tracy Lawrence told me that he almost got killed when he first moved to Nashville. After two men jumped him and his date on the way to a party, they persisted in telling him what they had planned to do to his lady friend. Tracy couldn't face this awful prospect and bravely decided to jump them. He was able to overpower the assailants, but not until after they had shot him.

"It took me a long time to get well, but I'm glad I did it." he said, rather modestly.

"You were a very brave hero," I added.

...

Trisha Yearwood's parents are educators, but they totally support their daughter's efforts to be a country singer.

"I'm very blessed," she told me, "to have parents who love me enough to believe in me."

...

Neil McCoy is probably one of the premier showman of all times. I enjoyed this young man thoroughly. His show was non-stop entertainment of the very best kind. He almost brought the house down with his "Beverly Hillbillies" rap song.

The next time Neil McCoy came to Dothan, I talked about what a fabulous entertainer he was on our show. I guess I did go on for awhile. Anyway, Neil McCoy was at a local motel watching us that morning.

That night when I went to do the interview with him, he spoke out very loudly, "Hey man, let that sweet lady come right on in, she really loves me!" Then he told me about hearing what I had said about him that morning on "The Morning Show."

...

One of my long dangling gold earrings popped off my ear while I was interviewing country star Marty Stuart. Like a true gentleman he was, he bent right down to pick it up for me. He never could get it back on my ear, but he tried. It surely added humor to our interview while he fiddled with the earring. Before the end of our visit, Marty told me about the genuine revival that was going on in Nashville. We also discussed the new trend in positive county music about true love and family values.

...

Another gifted artist who visited our "Morning Show" was the pianist "Dino". We showed some video clips of his big new show now being performed in Branson, Missouri. Before he left, he invited us to come up to see him as his guests.

...

I met Donna Douglas, who had been Ellie Mae Clampett , on the *Beverly Hillbillies* for a number of years, in Bonifay, Florida. Although she had aged a little, she was as vivacious as ever. Ms Douglas is now an inspirational speaker and singer. The local Bonifay residents stood in line for hours to get her autograph.

Donna Douglas told me that she was just at the right place at the right time when she got the role of "Ellie Mae."

"I do love critters," she enthusiastically stated. "Working on that show was a barrel of laughs. We were all like one big, happy family. I really hated to see it end."

Chapter Thirteen
WTVY News Four This Morning

At the beginning of this book, I related how the "Morning Show" had ended. When something ends, there is always a time of sadness. In this particular instance, I didn't have time to feel sad because as I explained earlier, "The Morning Show" ended on Friday, August 22nd and I started "WTVY News Four This Morning" on Monday, August 25th. It was wonderful to be back at my original time slot 7:00 - 8:00 a.m.

By the time I started on my new format, Joey Parker had moved on to WSFA - TV and Mary Hughes had returned to Columbus, Georgia. Jessica Clark was hired to join Mitch English at 6:00 a.m. in the mornings.

It was so good to have a team approach again, and I could have never chosen two more delightful co-workers than Jessica and Mitch.

Most people liked the new time slot even though they called to complain that I didn't have enough time. A few of our most loyal viewers didn't like the early time because they enjoyed sleeping late. All in all, most people can watch the program better now due to the earlier time.

I am still a night person, and I have to trick myself to get up every morning. I set my alarm 20 to 30 minutes early, and I push the "snooze" button many times before I can get up. Once I am up, however, I am fine. By the time

I get to WTVY, I am ready to do the show, "Sunny Side Up"!

Never before in my years on TV have I worked any harder to make sure I have the best quality interviews possible. I have less time now, so I have to make every second count.

Dr. Clint Rhynes, clinical psychologist for the Dozier School for Boys, has made numerous appearances on our new program to discuss everything from communicating with your teenager to discussions on the psychological mind-set of great historical figures during certain periods of their lives.

Attorney General Bill Pryor, Senator Jeff Sessions and Congressman Terry Everett visit our show often when they are in town. They keep us current on legislative affairs in Montgomery, as well as Washington, D. C.

We've added to our celebrity chefs with a cookbook author originally from Geneva, Al, Louise Thompson Childs; Kitty Killingsworth, former lunchroom supervisor from Slocomb; Valerie Bass from the Alabama Cattlemen's Association; Peter Thostensen, a businessman with Professional Business Partners; Pat Wright from "The Cracker Barrel"; Helen Jackson from Kelly's in Enterprise; and Lady Dietrich from Dietrich's Strawberry Farms.

...

Governor Zell Miller from Georgia, commissioned Judy Neal and her staff to produce videos to help teenagers in problem areas of their lives. One video dealt with teenage pregnancy, another discussed juvenile crime and the latest one entitled "Driving Ambition", handled the issue of teenage driving. All of the videos have won regional emmy awards because of the great quality of the production, and the effectiveness of the message to teens. Judy Neal has brought all of these videos to show portions of them on our program. Each time she visits, the impact is tremendous.

Anesthesiologist and Author, Dr. Fred Ernst, wrote *Now They Lay Me Down to Sleep* along with surgeon, Dr. William Pace. This book reveals all the answers to questions concerning what one needs to know before considering any type of surgery. Dr. Ernst was a guest on our show right after the book was published. I was also able to interview co-author Dr. William Pace before his death. Their work together continues to have far reaching effects on consumers everywhere as Dr. Ernst is invited to speak on hundreds of radio and television shows around the country, and is interviewed in all the print media to share this information.

Mary Heersink made an appearance on our program to tell about her son Damien's near-death experiance with e-coli bacteria. After eating a rare hamburger, the young boy became gravely ill. Mrs. Heersink's book about their family's ordeal has done much to inform the public about the dangers of e-coli. Mary Heersink has also done much nationally and internationally, as well, to change the way meat is processed.

Medical doctors like Dr. Sam Banner, from Nathanael Medical Center, discuss everything from proper testing procedures to the issue of flu shots. Anything dealing with health issues is always popular with our viewers.

Other professionals have included: Pediatrician Dr. Ted Williams who answers questions about infants and toddlers; Dr. Elizabeth Brogden, an eating disorder specialist from Canopy Cove in Tallahassee, Florida; Psycho-therapist Dr. Joan Kogelschatz who discussed "road rage", which is the alarming anger people are acting out on America's highways; Pain management specialist, Dr. J. Antonio Aldrete; Chicago-based neurosurgeon Dr. Ramsis Ghaly who shared with our viewers new help for chronic pain sufferers; Allergist Dr. Rufus Lee; Dermatologist Dr. Kelly Hood; and Dr. Tim Faulk who discussed the prevention of teenage suicide.

There have been so many other great medical and psychological professionals who have been special guests on our program that I could not possibly list them all. Our viewer response is tremendous each time we have a doctor in any field.

Fred Kelly, brother of legendary stage and screen star, Gene Kelly, has appeared on our program four times. Fred has shared stories about his brother's career as well as information on Hollywood's elite who have been taught to dance by one of the Kellys. For example, John Travolta started his dancing career with none other than Fred Kelly.

...

Human interest stories are always a plus for programming. Telling young Zack Sizemore's ordeal with a rare type of bone cancer, osteosarcoma, was one of my most touching interviews. After losing part of his leg, ever resilient Zack was later fitted with a unique kind of prosthesis which has allowed him to play sports again. Nothing seems to slow him down.

Some of our area's most outstanding artists, have also appeared on "WTVY News Four This Morning.," like Jeannie Maddox, Helen Taylor Andrews, Kathryn Smith, Rose Donahue and many others. The Dothan area is fortunate to have so much talent.

Joan Congdon brought her beautiful Fila Brasilero dogs to our show while her co-worker demonstrated their ability to protect their masters. My husband and I adopted one of her dogs which we named "Chief" (after Jerry Vann , whom I have always called "Chief".)

...

Two different mothers, Judith Hinton, whose daughter was murdered, and Molly Osteen whose son also was killed shared their stories on two separate shows that we aired. Neither one of the murders have ever been solved to this date.

The B Team Angels made a dramatic entrance on our program one morning. The concept was developed by some caring ladies in North Alabama as a ministry to shut-ins and those who are hospitalized. Members of the group dress in solid white with golden accents, haloes included. They were an instant hit! As a result of their visit to Dothan, our city now has our own chapter of the "B Team Angels".

...

Country artisans Pam and Tom Thompson not only provide us with a look at some of the most beautiful white oak baskets that they make, but they also bring a lot of their "country cousins" who also do unique and original "old timey" crafts. Tom is a true mountain man complete with a skunk hat and a wiry long beard. In spite of Tom's untamed humor, he and wife Pam still hold hands like newlyweds. They are truly refreshing individuals.

...

When the local Burger King chain began to lose business due to a national news story about an outbreak of ecoli-related illness, Helen Applefield, co-owner of the Dothan area franchise, came on our show to tell her story.

"We have never bought any of that type of beef believed to have caused the problem. The Burger King in question is in another state and has no connection to us in any way. So far, no one has ever gotten sick from eating our hamburgers." Ms Applefield insisted.

Her appeal must have worked because immediately after we aired her interview, Burger King hamburger sales began to pick back up.

...

One day a lady from the Ozark Health Food store brought along some Indian Corn that could be used to get ear wax out of one's ears. Mitch English agreed to let us demonstrate this on him. He put one side of his head on my coffee table while we poked the small end of the Indian corn in his exposed ear. Next, we lit the corn. It really works! Ear wax (or something) came out on the white sheet of paper that we had placed under Mitch's ear. That demonstration caused our phones to ring all day. Everyone wanted to try it. Dorothy Manning, WTVY's receptionist, threatened to make us answer all the calls because she was so swamped!

...

Many of our best programs have sparked controversy. One such issue was "Ways to bully-proof your school". My cousin's husband, Larry Hicks, principal of Carroll High School, shared some ways in which he had addressed this problem. Bravely, I tackled the dangers of aspartame, an artificial sweetener, with Betty Martini from Mission Possible International. Another hot topic was discussed via telephone with Phyllis Schlafly from "Eagle Forum" on the violence in American schools.

Pat Riley Jones, local representative from V.O.C.A.L., whose own mother was murdered, helped me secure many victims of crime to share their stories. None of them has been as unbelievable as Nancy Khan's. The woman who had been brutalized by a rapist-murderer, who left her for dead. Her story was made into a TV movie, as well as featured in the *Reader's Digest*.

During the horrible attack on Nancy, her cousin was cruelly tortured and murdered. Nancy, herself, survived only because after the rapist attempted to drown her, he tossed her body over a cliff. As Nancy's body hit the ground, the water was knocked out of her lungs and she regained consciousness. After coming to, she managed to claw herself back up the hill, only to discover the dead body of her cousin. Soon after this, she was able to flag a passing motorist and get some help. One of Nancy's eyes had been knocked out and the severity of her other wounds had left her in shock.

Although the perpetrator of this crime was finally apprehended and imprisoned, he is now eligible for parole. Every few years, Nancy has to go to his parole hearing to protest his release because this man has sworn to kill Nancy when he does get out. No wonder Nancy Khan, (now McCrary) works so hard for Victims of Crime and Leniency.

···

Dr. David Turok, ocular plastic surgeon, virtually re-did Leon Hutto's eyelids. Leon had been born with a birth defect which kept his top lids droopy and severely impaired his vision. Now, thanks to Dr. Turok's generosity and skill, Leon has a brighter future. Viewers loved the story.

···

Life is such a blessing and death appears to be such a remote thing to most of us. I certainly know that I wasn't thinking about dying or death when I interviewed the very talented twelve year old singer named Jenny Sky Sanders. The young girl stopped by WTVY to sing for us before leaving for Nashville to meet with Dolly Parton.

It was during the trip to *Music City USA* that Jenny suffered a severe asthmatic attack. Before her family could get her to the hospital, she had died.

As a memorial to Jenny, I did a special tribute to her and played one of her videos. Phone calls came in for hours after our show as viewers expressed their condolences over her death.

•••

Senior citizens have always been a big part of our program. Some of our strongest supporters have been members of the Burdeshaw-Soloman Senior Center in Headland, The Rose Hill Senior Center and the Cherokee Nutrition Center in Dothan. (I love and salute you all!)

•••

Former Dothan resident, Barbara Rich Jackson, stopped by one morning to review her new book, *For I heard Them Say Let Us Go to Dothan.* In her story, she depicted details on the life of her father, Mr. Van Rich, who opened the thriving department store for ladies in Dothan named appropriately, "Van Rich's". Ms Jackson also had priceless memories to share about the life of some of Dothan's earliest citizens.

•••

Fabulous area entertainers have performed for our viewers on our program such as the Enterprise State Junior College *Entertainers*, The Southeast Alabama Community Theater, Blakely, Georgia's *Early Editions*, *Opus Nostrum*, *Grits on the Side*, the cast of the Understudy Theater, the Southeast Alabama Dance Company, Colquitt, Georgia's cast members of *Swamp Gravy* and so many more. Individual soloists have shared their unique musical talents with us as well. Variety has been something that I have always strived to achieve on our show.

•••

Almost every subject there is, I have attempted to cover; such as, divorce recovery, overcoming grief, crime prevention, drug and alcohol abuse treatment programs (such as Teen Challenge and the Dothan-Houston County Substance Abuse Board),care for the mentally and physical challenged, educational opportunities from our area colleges (such as Wallace Community College, Enterprise State Junior College, Troy State University, Okaloosa-Walton State Technical College, Washington - Holmes Vocational Technical School and many others), care and protection of animals with our weekly "Pet of the Week" segments sponsored by the Wiregrass Humane Society, happenings at Dothan's Landmark Park and all the other wonderful organizations in our area. I could not begin to cover all the topics, subject matter or agencies that I have presented on our show through the years.

...

Every day has been a new challenge for me to achieve an even higher goal with programming. For example, only recently, I interviewed Barbara Joyner, Shirley Miles and Peggy Jackson who own Manna Foods and Manna Marketing. They believe God gave them a vision to sell their products , "Mimi's Southern Style Cornbread Dressing" and "My Mama's Chicken & Dumplings" to the American consumer, much in the same way Colonel Sanders perfected his Kentucky Fried Chicken enterprises. They not only promote their great food, but they are also market the artistic talents of Shirley and Peggy in inspirational literature. What an impact they have already made on my life and in the lives of all the others they have met.

...

Ponies, puppies, lions, exotic birds and even crocodiles have appeared on our program. A few months ago, two very spunky "crocs" were brought up from Orlando, Florida, by Tim Williams, a former alligator wrestler. It seems that a new addition to the Gatorland theme park, "Croc World", highlighting the world's largest crocodiles is opening near Disney World. One of Tim's crocodiles was about three feet long and very feisty. His mouth had to be taped. The other crocodile he brought was about twelve inches long. Tim told us that both of the reptiles were the same age.

"The difference," he explained, "is the feeding schedule. The larger crocodile gets fed daily while the smaller one is fed only twice a month."

I thought that Tim was being cruel to the tiny crocodile until he assured me that crocs in the wild can go for months without food.

"We do this to show our visitors crocs of various sizes. We have to keep some of them as pets." he grinned.

Jessica Clark walked into the lobby to meet Tim, not realizing what he had with him in the bag. Just as Jessica bent over to look, the restless crocodile stuck his head out and gave Jessica quite a scare.

"Not to worry," Tim exhorted us, Joan Lunden did worse than that when the croc I carried on "Good Morning America" startled her. She tossed one of the croc eggs that she was holding up in the air. After the commercial break," he concluded, "she apologized to the TV audience, and assured them that the broken egg had not been fertile."

Tim Williams even promised to come back to our show and bring his old friend, wildlife expert Jack Hanna, with him on his next visit. (Stay tuned.)

Chapter Fourteen
Miscellaneous Memories

There have been so many stories that I have failed to share in this book. I apologize if I have left someone out or have forgotten some incident that I should have remembered. This book is being written during my recuperation time from major surgery. Not many people have realized that I have been hospitalized because I was able to get most of my shows on tape before the scheduled date of my surgery.

I would especially like to thank our new WTVY manager, Pat Dalbey, and News director, Jeff Raker, for all their understanding and support during, before, and after this time of surgery. Special thanks also to my dear friend, Dorothy Manning, who is not only WTVY's capable receptionist, but also a special assistant to me. Dorothy has made sure that everything concerning our program and my other responsibilities have been taken care of while I was absent. She is a wonderful gift to me.

Huie Lee, Phillip Bump, Joe Holloway, Nathaniel Billins, Jessica Clark and Mitch English have also done their part to make sure every detail of the instructions I left were taken care of, so that our programming would move smoothly.

Our production department, under the leadership of Daniel Hamilton, co-operated with me in every way to make sure I could tape all the interviews that I needed to do before my surgery. How many times did I need and get an extra time for taping, I don't know. Thank you, Huie Lee, you never said "No!"

It is not easy for me to find a stopping place with this story because there is still so very much left to be told. (Perhaps, I feel a sequel coming on.) In this last chapter I have addressed some miscellaneous memories in order to coover a few more stories. Hope you enjoy these events also.

...

I have appeared on WTVY - TV for over 24 years and yet many, many viewers still call me "Betty". (Betty Gault was my predecessor, remember). One lady went so far as to stop me and my sister Paula at the Medical Center one day to tell me how much she loved our show. She went on to say, "I watch you every single day, Betty." (It took all my sister could do not to laugh out loud.)

Betty Gault also told me that for years after she took over "The Morning Show", people referred to her as "Barbara" (Barbara Gellersted Adams had been on WTVY right before Betty.)

...

Very soon after Rex Roach and I started working together, I had the chance to interview former LA Rams football star Roman Gabriel. This really made me a big star to my sister Becki Haston who had been "in love" with this athlete since her college days.

...

I know Charles Woods has a "forgiving heart". About two weeks after I started work at WTVY, he knocked on my office door. His hands were full, so, I jumped up to assist him in opening the door. As I rushed to his aid, my leg somehow got caught on the long telephone cord and I tripped, spilling the coffee I was carrying all over him and the papers in his arms. It appeared as if I had just deliberately thrown the entire cup at him. I was mortified. He was a little startled, I know, but he didn't fire me.

One morning, Mr. Woods asked me if I would like a promotion. Of course I said "Yes." He wanted me to work in the traffic department under Reggie Mitchell. Reggie logs in all the programming and commercials at WTVY.

I went to Reggie for advice.

"Ann, you can't possibly do traffic and work on your show at the same time." Reggie explained. "This is a job for a person who has to be sitting at their desk working on logs every minute of the day."

"What can I tell Mr. Woods?" I questioned.

"Tell him you don't want to do it," Reggie answered. "If you tell him you can't do it, he'll try to convince you that you can. Just tell him this job in not for you."

I took his advice and Mr. Woods said, "Okay." From then on if Mr. Woods asked me to do something out of my usual sphere of expertise, I said the same thing, "I don't want to do this." It always worked. Thank you, Reggie.

...

If I have seemed a little hard on Jerry Vann in this book it is because I truly love Jerry like a brother. Yes, he is a big tease and yes, he has mellowed quite a bit through the years. He is one of the people I most admire and respect at WTVY. After all he has worked for WTVY since August of 1958! He does deserve some respect. I do have two more Jerry Vann stories to tell before I end this book.

One night Jerry Vann called me at home many years ago. In his most business-like voice he inquired about the telethon that Chris Bence and I had co-hosted the previous spring.

"What about it, Jerry?" I asked.

When he went on to explain that a man was presently out at WTVY waving a gun and demanding an explanation as to what we had said about his Uncle Kelly on TV the night of the telethon, I didn't believe him.

By reason of the fact that Jerry has always been such a big kidder, it took awhile before he convinced me that he was telling the truth. To sum up: this poor man had watched us that night, and when I referred to Kelly Parker (a local beauty queen), the confused man thought we were talking about his own uncle who had the same name. He had evidently dwelled on it for months before he had decided to seek some answers. Thank goodness our Sheriff, A. B. Clark, was able to get the loaded gun away from him and take him to jail. We were told that the man had a serious mental problem (which did not lessen the danger our staff faced when he pulled the gun on them.)

I remember another time when Jerry called me at home because he needed a tape for the news that night. Since I had previously played the story on "The Morning Show", he had gone to my office to find it.

By the time I got Jerry's call, he was totally frustrated. My office was so small that I had no choice but to keep tapes stacked everywhere-on the floor-on my filing cabinet and anywhere else I could put them.

"Ann, I need that tape right now and there is no way in the world I can find it in this mess." Jerry grumbled.

"I know exactly where it is," I said. "Where are you now?" He told me that he was at my desk, so I told him to look straight ahead at my filing cabinet and that the second tape from the top in the stack nearest the edge was the one.

"You hold on," he ordered, obviously not believing me. When he found the tape right where I said it was, he came back to the phone in disbelief. "How did you possibly know where that tape was?" he demanded.

"I'm good", I laughed. "I'm just very good. I know where everything in my office is."

Jerry never knew(until he reads this, of course) that I had just sorted those tapes that very afternoon before he called me.)

...

On live TV, one never knows what to expect next. To illustrate, one morning right in the middle of the show, a very pregnant lady went into labor. I knew by looking at her that something was wrong. I called for a break, and then, we helped her get up off the couch. Her husband came out to the station and took her straight to the hospital. The baby was born a few hours later.

The local police got involved with one show on the morning an actor who depicted historical characters was arrested in our lobby right after he completed his performance. Someone had recognized the Florida native that day on the show and had notified authorities. The man was guilty of skipping out on his family and violating a court order to support his children.

John White later told me that I "owed" him for not arresting the actor on the air. "Oh no," I protested. "I wish you would have walked right in on the set to make the arrest. Think how great our ratings would have been after that?"

...

A Stradivarius violin is worth its weight in gold, I'm told. One day an elderly gentleman brought a genuine Stradivarius and a very expensive French violin out to show them on our program. He was looking for a buyer, he said. According to his story, he had acquired both violins from an Indian who had run up a huge bar tab at a club this man once owned.

Just as I was considering the irony of the poor Indian losing his prized violins due to his addiction to alcohol, all of a sudden, the elderly man made a terrible groan and appeared to be having a heart attack.

Our director, Joe Earl Holloway, had our cameraman Johnny Williford to zoom right in on the man. I was waving at our crew to do just the opposite. All I could think of at this point was to call for a commercial break, which I did. During our break, we discovered that the man had just undergone back surgery, and when he had moved toward me at one point, an excruciating pain had hit his back - hence, the groan! My next concern after discovering that the man had not suffered a heart attack was the possibility of someone seeing the show and trying to rob him of these priceless violins. I guess nothing happened to him after the show. At least we never heard about it if it did.

...

I can hardly believe the way some people dress these days. One bright morning, a very famous hair stylist from Atlanta brought two models with him to show off his newest hair designs. One was a very fair blonde, the other model was a stunning black woman. When the two of them walked out under our lights, it was very obvious that neither of them had on any underwear whatsoever. You could see right through their "clingy" long dresses! While my cameramen were staring at the women, I was giving them the signal to show <u>nothing</u> on the air but their heads and their hairstyles. I almost held my breath until the segment was over. Later, when the two women walked out past our next guests waiting in the lobby, there was silence until after they had left the building. Then, there was aloud commotion as varying exclamations were pronounced by our other visitors!

...

In the old building out on 52 East we were definitely lacking in any form of security system. One morning a very intoxicated man walked right in our back door. He described himself as a devoted fan of mine and to prove it, he had purchased me a pair of red, high-heeled shoes. Our cameramen tried to reason with him, but he just kept insisting that I take the shoes. We threatened to call the police unless he agreed to leave. He finally exited out the back door, but he left the red shoes behind.

...

No matter if I have been teased or even criticized sometimes, I have always tried to help people find their missing pets. One of my favorite stories of a pet recovery was the one about a missing dog who needed its heart medication. The distraught owner had called to tell us that her dog had run out of the gate in her fenced-in yard during a thunderstorm when the natural gas man had come to refill the tank. I took down all the information about the missing dog and announced it that morning on our show.

Later that night, a local preacher found the dog inside his church when he was getting ready for Wednesday night services. Remembering hearing about the missing dog on our show that morning, he called the TV station to get the owner's number.

No one knew how the dog had managed to get inside the church building, but the very happy owner explained that "at least he knew where to go to get help."

Eid Burgess, a beautiful oriental lady, credits us for the safe return of her beloved collie. So much so, as a matter of fact, that through the years she still calls to thank me.

...

Among my favorite things to do is introducing people. I have always been thankful that Don and Charlotte Lewis went to all the effort to help me meet my husband, Jerome, that I want to do the same for others. Two very happy couples that have met and married as a result of my introductions are: Jay Sample and Pam Boothe; and Myrtle Taylor and J. E. Speed.

I had done a story with Jay Sample on his technology to preserve the eroding beaches of America. Pam was a good friend of mine, and when they met, it was almost "love at first sight." They are still love-birds twelve years later.

J.E. Speed's wife had died of cancer a few months after I had aired a TV program about the Bonifay Nursing Home that they owned. Janie Bush, a saleslady for WTVY-FM, told me that Mr. Speed was grieving terribly over the loss of his beloved wife. I decided to take him out to lunch in an effort to cheer him up.

Right after our luncheon, I had to leave for my skin care appointment with Myrtle Taylor at the Kutt Above. It was during my facial that the idea hit me. Myrtle herself was a widow!

When I told Myrtle of my plan for her to meet Mr. Speed, she was not at all in favor of it at first. I think she was just a little shy. At last, over Myrtle's protests, Janie and I managed to introduce them. Their marriage was truly a wonderful one. "Speed," as she affectionately called him, and Myrtle lived happily together for seven years until his death. "Those were the happiest years of my life," she confided in me later.

...

Mail has always been important to me. I appreciate viewers for writing to express their opinions . One letter, in particular, meant a great deal to me. The lady who wrote to me thanked me for being the means that God had used to restore her husband's will to live for a number of years.

Even though he had eventually died, for over eight years, he had faithfully watched our show.

As she further explained in the letter, when her husband had first suffered a stroke, he was so depressed that he had simply given up his will to live. He lay with his back to her and turned his face to the wall. He even refused to try to get up.

One morning she got the idea for me to wish him a "Happy Birthday" on his birthday. He still refused to get up when she told him of her plans. He really didn't believe her, I guess. When all of his friends began to call to tell him what I had done, he was greatly surprised.

Because he still wouldn't get up, his wife had called me again. This time, I spoke directly to him the next morning, teasing him in a "scolding tone" about not even getting up to see me wish him a "Happy Birthday". I went on to say that he'd better start watching our show because there was no telling what I would say about him next.

When she told him what I had said, he finally got up to watch. From then on she said he would get up every morning and say, "We'd better go watch Ann, there's no telling what she might say about me next."

To my knowledge I never mentioned his name again, but according to his wife, he had remained one of our most faithful viewers until his death.

She had ended her letter with, "Thank you for giving me back my husband for his last remaining years."

What a blessing to me that letter has become. You never know that what you say or do can so affect the lives of others.

...

A young boy who was suffering from an eating disorder had asked to meet me and Gene Ragan. His parents had called us because they hoped we might be able to help him. We spent thirty minutes or more with him trying to get him to start eating again. I will always hope we did some good.

I also visited a very handsome young man who was dying with aids. As I neared his bed, he sat up and threw his arms around me. I didn't want him to sense any rejection on my part, but truthfully, I was a little frightened. I had not been educated very much about aids at the time. I did my best, with my limited knowledge, to give him some hope. He allowed me to pray for him before I left, but he eventually died from this dread disease.

...

A very troubled mother called me at the TV station to ask me to go pray for her son who was in a coma. I went to the hospital and was allowed to go into an intensive care unit to pray for the young man who had suffered injuries in a motorcycle accident. He really looked bad. He was swollen, black and blue, and had stitches all over his face and body.

As I prayed for God to bring him back, a hand touched my shoulder. It gave me such a start that I yelled! (It was one of his friends who was letting me know that he was joining in the prayer.) In a few days after this, the patient, who had been in a coma, came out of it and is well today. (Maybe the prayer and the yell helped.)

...

I have been very fortunate to be able to travel quite a bit during the twenty-four years that I have worked at WTVY. On a trip to San Diego, my daughter Paige and I ran into Jerry Clower, whom I had previously interviewed at least two different times. When I introduced my daughter to him, he gruffly said, "Don't you ever get into trouble, honey, cause your mama sure couldn't deny you!"

...

As a result of various contests held on our "Morning Show", Jerome and I have been able to cruise to Nassau and Alaska as escorts to two different groups of travelers. We have both enjoyed interacting with new friends who we have been able to meet because of these opportunities. Myra Ishler from Odyssey Tours and Travel has been very instrumental in arranging all of these tours.

...

While my children were growing up, I always arranged to take them out one at a time for an individual outing or "date". Once, my son Trant wanted to eat at Wiener King. Just about the time I had bitten off a big chunk of a footlong hotdog, a very excited viewer spotted me as she was passing by our table. In her enthusiasm, she reached over to hug me. As she did, she pulled my chin up causing me to "choke" on my hotdog.

Even as tears were streaming down my face while I struggled to get the chunk of food down, she never realized what had happened. The overjoyed viewer just went on and on about how much she loved our show. It was a miracle that I was finally able to swallow the hotdog when she decided to go find a place to sit.

...

I was also mobbed once in a local department store by a family of ten who "watched me every day," they said. I got so many hugs and kisses I couldn't believe it. It embarrassed my children, but it didn't really bother me.

...

A young girl who was staring at me in Wal-Mart one Saturday morning looked at me and said, "You're not Ann Varnum." (I guess she couldn't believe I was wearing bluejeans and a pullover.)

"Well," I answered, "I surely try to be!"

...

"God even answers prayers about dogs," I said to one of my cameramen, Terry Key, right after we both witnessed a miracle. Terry and I were on the way back from taping some interviews when we looked up and saw a big truck about to hit a beautiful dog. I immediately cried out, "Lord, please save that dog!"

Terry and I both watched the truck run right over the dog. In awe, we watched the dog get up, shake himself and run off into the woods. I still don't know what happened, but I was so happy that it did.

...

Kombiz Noori was from Iran. Mr. Woods gave him a job as a cameraman. He worked very hard to be a good employee and to try to fit into our culture. Every morning as a sign of respect to me he would offer to kiss my hand. I finally convinced him that in America a hug or handshake was sufficient. Kombiz did his own version of our American "hug." He would walk over to me and place his head on my shoulder like an affectionate child. It was awkward at first, but I learned to appreciate his "hug" and especially, Kombiz himself.

Vinnie Fusco is now the director of the Monteil Williams Show. He started his career at WTVY right after college. The day Vinnie came to work, I happened to overhear him on the telephone trying to find a place that would allow him to stay on credit until he could get his first paycheck. I stepped in and insisted that he come home with me. He couldn't believe this "Southern hospitality", as he called it. After meeting this young man, our two sons immediately became good friends with him. He remained at our house until we found him a place to live. Vinnie Fusco came to us with long, scraggly hair and a grizzled beard, wearing faded, torn jeans. When I saw him recently, his hair is stylishly short, and his attire - strickly modern chic. His talent has taken him to the top. Vinnie still calls, nevertheless, from time to time, to check up on me.

...

When Aaron Tippin came to town, he was already a big country star. Scheduled to make an appearance at the National Peanut Festival, Mr. Tippin stopped by WTVY - FM to promote his big show. When I attempted to get an interview with him, his road manager very rudely said, "We don't have time!" and hurried Mr. Tippin into the elevator. Knowing the history of Aaron Tippin's musical career, I called the one person who had helped him get started - my very close friend, Charlie Monk, in Nashville.

After telling my experience to Charlie, he simply asked, "Where is he now?" I told him. Then he assured me, "Don't worry, darling, I'll handle it."

In less than ten minutes, the road manager was back in my office apologizing to me and inviting me to please come up to the radio station to do my interview.

Aaron Tippin, himself, was a very nice man. Charlie had also earlier filled me in on some inside information about Mr. Tippin which gave me a different slant for an interview. It was well worth my efforts, and, after all, I had already promised our viewers that Aaron Tippin would be my special guest the next day on "The Morning Show". So, he was.

...

The only time I had a guest to suddenly switch subjects on me was the time urologist Dr. Lamar Miller decided to discuss sexual dysfunction in men instead of the planned topic of lithotripsy. I had only a few minutes to adjust to the new topic before air time.

Dr. Miller even brought out the implant that was now being used to help restore a man's potency. Since call-ins were planned already, I had to remind my cameramen that this was to be a serious issue, with no room for jokes or silly remarks.

In spite of the unusual subject matter, Dr. Miller handled the topic remarkably well. It was a first for me, but today, the question of male sexual dysfunction is discussed routinely on television and elsewhere.

· · ·

With all our call-ins, there was only one incidence of an indecent remark being made over the air. It happened during a sewing segment. A gravelly voice called in to pose a vulgar request to my guest. Had she not responded with such indignation, I could have probably covered the whole thing up, and viewers would not have realized what he had said.

As for me, I did not react to the caller except to reach over and press the button on the phone in order to take the next question.

Public response to what had happened, was encouraging. Our loyal viewers were outraged over the man's call, and some even suggested "taking care" of him for me if they could ever find him. (Things do have a way of working out.)

· · ·

Young De Wayne Brown had leukemia and the only hope for his survival was a bone marrow transplant. The entire city helped to raise funds for his treatment. When the money was secured and it was time to go to the hospital, his younger brother, Brandon, gave DeWayne some of his own healthy bone marrow. That was another story I'll never forget.

· · ·

Lovely, single mother, Hope Tindell Wray, is another case where people from the entire area worked to help her get the medical treatment that she needed. Paralyzed virtually from the waist down due to a debilitating illness, limb-girdle muscular dystrophy, Hope's only chance for improvement was to receive an experimental series of injections which insurance still did not cover. Hope has now received those treatments, and we are waiting for the results.

···

Charles Woods' generosity has resulted in the development of Meadow Wood Inc., a non-profit Christian Life Adventure Camp which my husband and I have helped to form along with an excellent board of directors. The land had originally been a girl scout camp, but when the Girl Scout organization decided to no longer hold camping activities there, the land was returned to Charles Woods.

"When I was a little boy," Mr. Woods told us, "I always wanted to go camping, and I never got to go. I want little boys and girls to always be able to go camping if they want to, whether they have the money or not."

In addition to Meadow Wood, Providence Christian School has been built on the front part of the property there. It is a school which features an accelerated classical education based on Christian values.

···

There have been many very talented women who have come to work in WTVY's news department. A large number of them have moved on to an even bigger opportunity after leaving our station. Some have given up their careers in favor of becoming full-time wives and mothers. All of these ladies have been unusually gifted, but I have come to love and appreciate, in a far more personal way, the ones who have become a part of my Monday night Bible study which meets in my home.

"My girls," as I call them, have included: Carrie Deloney Givins, Brenda Sando Payne, Michile Smith Lam, and most recently, Jessica Clark and Andrea Emery. Julia Blackwell, personal assistant to our station manager, Pat Dalbey, is also a regular member. As an older woman, it has been an honor to watch these younger women grow in their faith and confidence in the Lord.

...

Dana Andrews has always been one of my favorite actors. He was in Dothan to speak to a group sponsored by Wiregrass Mental Health on drug and alcohol abuse prevention. When Mr. Andrews walked in to our studio ten minutes before air time, he demanded a make-up artist. I rushed to my own make-up supply and did the best I could with his face. Just as I finished, we were on the air.

While he was being interviewed, he talked about his own battle with alcohol. His story was very moving as he related all of the events which led up, finally, to his seeking help. We were just beginning to talk about Alcoholics Anonymous when our director called for a break.

As soon as the commercial time was up, I re-established where we had been in the interview, but for some reason the actor never made the connection that we were back on "live". He just kept on talking about, "All that blarney about faith in God. I never bought it for a minute. There is no God! My father was a minister, but he didn't believe it either." Mr. Andrews expounded.

I knew I had to get out of this one as it was evident that he didn't know we were actually "on the air", so I called for still another break.

When he realized he had made those remarks on television, all he did was shyly smile and say "oops!"

At my request, Dana Andrews gave me his address. I later wrote him a letter to share my own belief in God. Whether he ever read it or not, or whether it made a difference in his life or not, I don't know. I only know I had to try. Dana Andrews was found dead in his home a very short time later.

...
And the story continues…..

Chapter Fifteen
Excerpts from Letters and Memos

29 August 1980

Dear Ann:

I have always liked to be on the front line and I feel I am back there again in this new job in Saudi Arabia. It just happens that the Middle East is once again in the forefront of the news and in our strategic thinking...

Here is what I am doing here. I came here from Louisiana to be Managing Director of Arabian Helicopters, Ltd... AHL is the only big helicopter operation in the country...

For now I should close by telling you that I leave Saturday Night for London to meet Jaye and attend the Farnsborough Air show. I will be back here on the front line a week later. I hope this finds you, Jerome and Charles Woods in good health and spirits. Please give them and your viewers my very best.

Sincerely,
Bill
William J. Maddox, Jr.

January 24, 1981

Dear Ann:

Thank you for your invitation to visit with the wonderful people of Dothan and Houston county. "You-all" were just great on my earlier campaign visits - you especially with your good TV show!

Sincerely,
Jerimiah A. Denton, *Jr.*

Dear Annie,

I have just a few minutes here after the news to sit down and drop you a line to say that all's well in Montgomery. How about Dothan? I haven't had a whole lot of time to write letters, but I did want to scratch out a few lines to you...Cause you're special.

How are the following: you, Jerome, the kids, the dogs, the TV station, Jerry Vann, Al Roberts, Doodle, Steve, etc.

People up here are amazed at some of the stories I tell about working at WTVY.

...

Let me hear from you. Much love and all that good stuff...

Bob Howell
WSFA – TV News Anchor

SATURDAY AFTERNOON
JUNE 24, 1989

DEAR ANN:
...

ON BEHALF OF SELMA STREET SCHOOL, I WOULD LIKE TO EXPRESS MY APPRECIATION TO YOU, AND THE STATION'S STAFF FOR THE EXCELLENT COVERAGE OF SELMA STREET'S CHRISTMAS OPEN HOUSE.

THANKS FOR HAVING BEEN A "LIGHT" IN OUR COMMUNITY FOR MANY YEARS IN THE PAST AND, HOPEFULLY, MANY YEARS TO COME. YOUR WARMTH AND COMPASSION FOR PEOPLE CERTAINLY ADD MUCH TO WTVY'S PROGRAMMING.

ROGER O. SMITH
PRINCIPAL
SELMA STREET SCHOOL

11-18-92

Dear Ann:
I cannot go on your program and I am so sorry that I can't. I am not allowed to drive a car, my 5 day nurse drives for me....

Well I wish I could make it but I just can't. Please write me about your family. God Bless you and hold you close in His arms.

Try me again when I am 20 years younger.
I Love You,
Harry
(Harry Hall)

"Sunny Side Up"

May 16, 1990

Dear Ann:

Well what a good sport you are! I really enjoyed being on your morning television show. You are quite a legend in Alabama and now I know why. So many people came to the mall and said they saw us together on your show. Again, thanks for making my visit to Dothan so special. I wish you continued health and happiness.

> Love,
> Richard
> (Richard Simmons)

MEMO:

I'm sorry I missed you. It seems I only come when you're not here. I think of you often. Please do the same. I'll love you always.

> Henry
> (Henry Nance)

One of my cameramen that I had the privilege of leading to Christ

Hi!

We are having a wonderful time, weather is beautiful, and your mission has been accomplished. (Thank you so much) Don't expect the honeymoon to ever end. We love you so much.

> Myrtle & Speed

The couple I introduced.

THE WHITE HOUSE

WASHINGTON

December 14, 1982

Dear Mrs. Varnum:

Thanks so much for your message of encouragement. When I hear from someone like you I am filled with a renewed sense of dedication. To lead and serve such Americans is an honor beyond comparison. I am deeply grateful for you heartening words, and especially for your prayers. I hope I will be worthy of your continuing support.

Nancy joins me in wishing you and your loved ones all the joys and blessings of the Holy Season of Christmas. May they be with you throughout the new year!

Sincerely,

Ronald Reagan

Mrs. Ann Varnum
Post Office Box 1089
Dothan, Alabama 36302

Dear Ann,

It took a little time, but here is the hat you requested in Atlanta.

This is not something John does for 'just anyone and everyone,' but I told him how much it would mean to your friend with the hat collection.

I hope we meet again. I once lived in Choctawhatchee Wells, Alabama, and visited Dothan and environs.

Yours,

Lou

Lou Vipperman

For

JOHN HILLERMAN

Thanks, Neighbor

Dear Editor,

As citizens of Enterprise I feel it appropriate to write an open letter of thanks to WTVY-TV for the "Morning Show" with Ann Varnum. She is so willing and personable to allow so many of our Enterprise folks to be on her show.

WTVY-TV's interest in Enterprise activities is just what I call being a "good neighbor!"

Thanks,
Hilda Forehand

THE WHITE HOUSE
WASHINGTON

January 6, 1993

Dear Ms. Varnum:

Thank you so much for your warm expression of sympathy. It
means a lot to the entire Bush Family. It means a lot to the
entire Bush family. Dorothy Walker Bush was a caring and kind
person and a loving mother, and we will miss her.

We also appreciate your words of encouragement. While victory
was not meant to be, Barbara and I are grateful for so many
blessings – among them our family and wonderful supporters.
We will always be grateful for the privilege that we have had of
serving the American people.

Best wishes.

Sincerely,

George Bush

Ms. Ann Varnum
Director, Public Relations
WTVY-TV4
Post Office Box 1089
Dothan, Alabama 36302

"Sunny Side Up"

MEMO:
SUBJECT : FISHING BOAT IN PARKING LOT
TO : PRODUCTION MAMAGER
FROM : NEWS DIRECTOR

   DEAR MR. FINN.
  I BELIEVE THE FISHING BOAT HOOKED TO THE REAR OF
DIRECTOR JOE EARL HALLOWAY,S CAR WILL HAVE A BAD EFFECT
ON EVERYONE WORKING AT WTVY ESPECIALLY THE NEWS DEPT.
WHERE WE HAVE TO WORK LONG HARD HOURS. . . THE #%*#&*
BOAT WILL ONLY REMIND THE NEWS DEPT. THAT WE DO NOT HAVE
TIME TO GO FISHING NOR THE MONEY TO BUY A FISHING BOAT.
  I BELIEVE THIS XXX SHIP SHOULD BE HIDDEN MAYBE BEHIND
THE WAREHOUSE. . . AND MR. HALLOWAY SHOULD BE OBSERVED
VERY CLOSELLY, SINCE HE HAS TO WORK THE RED HOLLAND SHOW
FIVE DAYS PER WEEK,,,, HE MAY HAVE CONTACTED RED HOLLAND
DISEASE. . IF HE SHOULD BEGIN TALKING IN A LOUD MANNER
AND USUING PHRASE,9 (THREY'RE TEARING IT UP OVER AT THE
RIVER) YOU MAY HAVE TO PERSCRIBE R AND R FOR HIM.

        JERRY VANN
        NEWS DIRECTOR

    ANN HERE IS TAPES OF THE BIG HAT EVENT, THE EDITED
TAPE IS ABOUT 2 MIN, AND TWENTY SECONDS ,IT HAS SOUND ALL
YOU NEED TO DO IS INTRO   IT WITH SOMETHING LIKE THIS. .
THE MAD HATTIER WAS HELD YESTERDAY   IN DOTHAN FOR THE
BENEFIT OF XXXXX THE AMERICAN CANCER SOCIETY. . . . TWO
EVERNTS WERE HELD AT THE RAMADA INN, HERE ARE SOME SCENES
FRON YESTERDAY,S NOON LUNCHEON.   FEATURING MODELS FROM
GAYFFEERS, HATX,S FROM LOCAL LADIES AND TALENT FROM SOME
LITTLE KID WHO WILL GROW UP TO EAT JELELY DONOUGHTS AND
BE ANOTHER ELVIS. . .   THE CHIEF
        JERRY VANN

(Reproduced in the exact form as the original memos.)

DEAR ANN HERE IS A FORTY SECOND TAPE OF SANTA CLAUS XXXX ASKING EVERYONE TOCOME TO DOTHAN,S CHRISTMAS PARADE THIS MONDAYNIGHT. . .THE PARADE IS SPONSORED BY THE CENTURIONCLUB AND THE CITY OF DOTHAN . . . THIS WILL BE THE BIGGEST AND BEST EVER . . . THERE WILL EVEN BE EIGHT LIGHTED FLOATES, AND WTVY WILL HAVE A FLOAT IN THE PARADE, THE PARADE WILL START AT PORTER SQUARE MALL AND TRAVEL EAST ON MAIN TO POPLAR HEAD PARK THEN THE CHRISTMAS TREE WILL BE OIT , THERE WILL BE SINGING AND AN INSPIRIATIONAL MESSAGE FROM PAUL ESTES. . . .ADND SANTA CAN TALK WITH KIDS. . .STARTS A SIX THIS MONDAY NIGHT. . .ALSO THEY WANTED YOU TO RIDE ON OUR FLOAT. . .SEE BECKEY. . .JERRY VANN   P.S. I TYPED THIS WITHOUT MY GLASSES

ann here is a two minute tape i hope you can run on monday, s show. . .you need to have director play silent night underneath while you talk,,,i repeat it has no sound. . . .the first forty seconds is shots inside xxxxlafayettee st. methodist showing their christmas decorations,,,,,,you might compliment all churchs in the wiregrass since they all go out in a big way for the season they all have special musical events all designed to honor the true meaning of christmas .. not just toy,s under the tree and what am i going to get9by the way what has jerome recieved that you are going to give away, xxx i can,t beleive he don,t miss all that stuff) but i,m sure you will know what to say. . .the last onem inute and twenty seconds is a scene at evergreen prepsterian. . .they will have theirs up xxxxxx through tomorrow night they are using kids from the church,,,in rotation. . . .9 (SORRY I HAD TO FEATURE METHODISTS AND PREPSTERIANS,,,ICAN,T SPELL))   (BUT YOU KNOW WHAT YOU SAID GOD LOVES EVERYBODY, EVEN NEWS PEOPLE)
JERRY VANN
P.S... MAKE SURED THEY GET UP SILENT NIGHT

WTVY-FM
95.5 MHZ
DOTHAN, ALABAMA
36301

RADIO

ANN, THE TAPE IS READY TO GO ITS CUED UP AND REALLY SOUNDS GOOD SO SOCK IT TO EM. SEE YOU LATER THIS MORNING.

NOT BEING INFORMED TO THE
HIGHTEST DEGREE OF ACCURACY,
I HESITATE TO ARTICULATE
FOR FEAR THAT I MAY DEVIATE
FROM THE TRUE COURSE OF
RECTITUDE.

SAMMY FAULK

DEAR AUBURN MORNING SHOW PERSONS:
THIS IS TO INFORM YOU THAT I WILL BE THE OFFICIAL MORNING SHOW ALABAMA PERSON BY PROXY. I DO NOT BELIEVE THE MILLIONS,

HUNDREDS OF THOUSANDS, THOUSANDS, THE GREAT NUMBER OF ALABAMA FANS IN THE TELEVISION AUDIENCE WOULD BE TREATED FAIRLY WITH ONE OF YOU REPRESENTING THEIR INTERESTS.

THERE-FORE I, INTREPID FOLLOWER OF THE SACRED BEAR-PERSON AND CRIMSON PACIDERM (sp?) SHALL BECOME THE DEFENDER OF BAMA-ISM (IN SPIRIT IF NOT IN PERSON) AND RALLY TO THE CAUSE OF ALABAMAISTS IN ORDER TO PRESERVE THE MIGHTY RIVALRY THAT EXISTS BETWEEN THE VALIANT RED AND WHITE AND THOSE OTHER TWO COLORS ON THE RAINY PLAINS.

CORDIALLY YOURS IN BAMAISM,

SIR BOB OF BAMA
DUKE OF HOWELL
RULER OF ALL GARDENIA
MARTER OF CANINES
CONQUEROR OF MONONUCLEOSIS
AND ALL AROUND GOOD GUY.

(Sent to Ann Varnum and Rex Roach by Bob Howell.)

ANN:

YOU HAVE BEEN THE BEST PART OF MY INVOLVEMENT AT WTVY-TV.

DURING THE HARD TIMES, WHEN I DIDN'T THINK I'D BE ABLE TO HOLD OUT, GOD SPOKE TO ME THROUGH YOU.

YOU HAVE ALSO BEEN HERE TO SHARE THE GREAT TIMES OF TRIUMPH THAT I'VE BEEN BLESSED TO BE A PART OF.

YOU ARE AN EXAMPLE OF CHRIST'S LOVE. YOU ARE A COUNSELOR, A MENTOR AND A FRIEND. WELL, YOU'RE "GRANNIE ANNIE!"

THANK YOU FOR ALL...I LOVE YOU, ANN.

In Him,

Tony '97

_____**joey m. parker**_____

Rex Roach

Bob Howell　　　**Ann Varnum**　　　**Bill Espy**　　　**Jim Houghton**

Don Day   **Ann Varnum**   **Sam Elliot**

**Tony Scott, Ann Varnum
and The Ft. Rucker 49'er Party**

The New Morning Show
WEEKDAYS at 7AM with
ANN VARNUM & CHRIS BENCE

WTVY TV 4 Dothan

Ann Varnum   **Teresa Thomas**   **Tom Nebel**

THE MORNING SHOW

Teresa	Ann	Gary
Thomas	Varnum	Bruce